## VOL. 7: GAAV'S CHALLENGE

### WRITTEN BY
### HAJIME KANZAKA

### ILLUSTRATED BY
### RUI ARAIZUMI

**HAMBURG // LONDON // LOS ANGELES // TOKYO**

*Slayers Vol. 7: Gaav's Challenge*
Written by Hajime Kanzaka
Illustrated by Rui Araizumi

Translation - Jeremiah Bourque
English Adaptation - Lianne Sentar
Layout Artist - Courtney H. Geter
Cover Design - Christopher Tjalsma
Editor - Kara Allison Stambach

Senior Editor - Jenna Winterberg
Pre-Production Supervisor - Erika Terriquez
Digital Imaging Manager - Chris Buford
Production Manager - Liz Brizzi
Managing Editor - Vy Nguyen
Creative Director - Anne Marie Horne
Editor in Chief - Rob Tokar
Publisher - Mike Kiley
President and COO - John Parker
CEO and Chief Creative Officer - Stuart Levy

A  Novel

TOKYOPOP Inc.
5900 Wilshire Blvd. Suite 2000
Los Angeles, CA 90036

E-mail: info@TOKYOPOP.com
Come visit us online at www.TOKYOPOP.com

ISBN: 978-1-4278-0504-1

First TOKYOPOP printing: January 2008
10 9 8 7 6 5 4 3 2 1
Printed in USA

# CONTENTS

# 1: DARK CLOUDS OVER DOWNTOWN DILSE

Flashes tore through the night woods, drenching the trees with light and throwing long, tangled shadows out across the littered forest floor.

I dove. Something flared up right where I'd been standing a second earlier, confirming that diving had been a good idea. I rolled to my knees and turned just in time to see a clutch of trees in that burst of light disappear into thin air.

. . . *Yikes*. I grimaced. It looked like that thing *was* after me.

And what was I doing there, you may ask? Why was I running through a forest in the middle of the night from some badass, mysterious enemy who wanted nothing more than to vaporize me, maybe even wipe me off the face of the planet?

Again?

Before you can say anything, I didn't ask for it this time. Seriously. I was staying in a small inn in a small village, minding my own business (and trying to catch some shut-eye for a change), and then this new Lina-hater-of-the-day came out of nowhere and attacked me. Out of nowhere! Seriously! And I didn't rob anyone or insult anyone or kick the crap out of anyone!

. . . Again.

So you can understand why I was a little shocked by the whole thing. But Lina Inverse stays cool in even the most undeserved and random of fights, so I (gracefully) fell out of bed, evaded the attack, and bolted out of the village as fast as possible. I knew that if I could lure that prick out to the neighboring forest, I could use the best magic I had without destroying a hell of a lot of public property.

Still, as I stared at that white, misty silhouette ducking around trees in the woods, I couldn't help but think that my spectacular plan might need some adjusting. This wasn't some bandit or common lowlife I was dealing with; there was a good chance that a lot of my spells, even my *really awesome* spells, would do me little to no good.

I was up against a Mazoku. Since those guys feed off darkness, spells that affect the living bounce right off them.

I needed a new plan. I quickly chanted and released a spell before that silhouette could get uncomfortably close.

"Elmekia Lance!" I shouted.

Just before my arrow of white light could impale him, the silhouette melted into the ground. The white shadow snaked across the ground as my spell passed harmlessly over what looked like his head.

*Dammit.* I gritted my teeth and shifted my feet. It looked like it was going to be a long night.

Just then, someone in the nearby darkness released some very promising Power Words.

"Ra Tilt!"

FWOOOM!

The misty demon was instantly enveloped in a pillar of blue light. The light blazed for a second, throwing my shadow out far behind me, then vanished as quickly as it had come. The demon was nowhere to be found.

I let out a relieved sigh. Dusting the dirt off my knees, I called out to the friendly caster. "Thanks, Amelia."

"Don't thank me yet," she called back.

I looked up. The nearby thicket rustled as Amelia pushed her way out of it, her dark hair barely reflecting the moonlight. But what surprised me more than her slightly-less-dramatic-than-usual entrance was the look of concern on her face.

"Something else is here," she murmured, her eyes darting around the area.

"Something *else?*" I followed suit and started scanning the surrounding darkness, my mind quickly going alert. If Amelia said she felt something, you could bet something was there. Amelia had been traveling with me for a while, and if I'd learned one thing about her—other than the fact that she's a nut about justice and she likes to scream about it as much as possible—it was that her priestess nature could let her sense things that I had no way of knowing.

Case in point: I didn't feel the presence of anyone at that moment, and the only thing I heard was the chirping of insects. But if Amelia felt something, then I wasn't about to . . .

My train of thought died the second the insects went silent.

"Hmm," came a familiar voice from behind Amelia and me. "I'd meant to hide my presence. You certainly are attentive."

I whipped around. A smiling old man, his white hair neatly combed back, emerged from the darkness. He looked simultaneously non-threatening and forgettable, but Amelia and I knew better. My blood ran cold.

"Raltaak," I muttered, beads of sweats forming on my forehead.

Despite the granddaddy look, the guy was a Mazoku—and a pretty high-ranking one, if my hunch was right. Amelia and I had gotten a taste of his power when he'd summoned a horde of low-ranking demons from the Astral Plane to posses a bunch of animals and create a small army of lesser demons. I wasn't sure how much power the guy really had, but I didn't want to find out.

*Not that fleeing's gonna work,* I reminded myself. I didn't want to fight Raltaak head-on, but I doubted he would just let me duck out and go back to bed.

"I think I get it now," I said carefully. "That white thing was just bait to get me out here, huh?"

"Not at all," Raltaak answered. He smiled awkwardly and shook his head. "I was expecting him to defeat you. Of course, I was ready to step in and finish the job if he wasn't sufficient, but the young lady over there noticed me." He glanced at Amelia momentarily. "And so quickly and easily—I'm surprised."

"Attacking an inn out of the blue isn't your style," I retorted. "Not from what I've seen, anyway."

"I won't harm the uninvolved. But, well . . ." Raltaak shrugged. "I have special circumstances."

*Circumstances.* I resisted the urge to roll my eyes. *Thanks for clearing that up.*

"Either way," Raltaak continued, making a deep, pained smile. "I'll eliminate you, no matter the—"

CHOOM!

Every hair on my body stood on end. Raltaak, his mouth still open to say his piece, suddenly slammed his jaw shut.

Twisted bloodlust, a kind far beyond the capacity of a human being, filled the area like a thick, invisible fog. The feeling enveloped me so tightly that I choked.

But the real cincher was that it *wasn't* coming from Raltaak.

"What?!" Amelia yelped. She whipped around in circles, obviously trying to find the source.

That was when Raltaak, the insanely powerful bad guy Mazoku, cried out in fear. I could see him shaking as he retreated into the darkness like a terrified puppy.

The bloodlust suddenly vanished, as if following the guy.

*Uh . . . whoa.*

Amelia and I just stood there for a second, completely dumbfounded. I noticed the thin sheen of sweat on her—at least I wasn't the only one ready to nearly wet my pants at the whole thing.

"Wh-what was that just now?" Amelia whispered in a broken voice.

I swallowed and shook my head. "Beats me," I murmured, but I had my suspicions as to who had caused that bloodlust.

Xelloss. If Raltaak had high-tailed it because of bloodlust alone, it *had* to have been Xelloss.

I glanced at Amelia. I hadn't told her (or anyone) that the mysterious priest who tended to tag along on adventures and always insisted on a single room was a servant of Greater Beast Zelas Metallium. Since Metallium was one of Ruby Eye's retainers, that made Xelloss almost stupidly powerful. It had become our little secret.

For whatever reason, unlike Raltaak and his goons, Xelloss was "protecting" me. Not out of the goodness of his heart, I'm sure, but it still meant a quick way out of tight spots like that evening. I didn't know what Xelloss' expectations were, but I still had to play along—no matter how disconcerting.

Amelia sighed and wiped her forehead. "Whatever the case," she murmured. "It looks like we made it through this one."

"Looks like it." I turned toward the village, my mantle fluttering out behind me. "Wanna go back to the inn?"

It was only then that I noticed the distant cries of Gourry and Zelgadiss. From the sound of it, they were running into the woods to find out where we'd disappeared.

*Some help* they *were,* I thought with mild distaste. I cleared my throat and shook out my cape. *But Lina Inverse needs no aid.*

***

"So?" Zelgadiss asked the next morning. His eyes peered at me, the only part of his face visible from behind his usual white scarf.

"So what?" I asked, keeping up my pace along the highway. I like to be efficient—walking and talking saves time.

Zelgadiss' stare went darker. "So, what happened to Xelloss?" he clarified.

I very nearly lost that traveling efficiency when my body tried to screech to a halt. But I'm more composed than that, so my shock was reduced to the brief hesitation of a single step.

*Ha!* I thought. *Take that, feelings!*

"Oh, you know Xelloss," I said with a dismissive wave of my hand. "He appears, he disappears—really, who can keep track of anyone these days?"

Zelgadiss was still staring at me, so I averted my eyes from his gaze. Okay, so maybe I had a guess why we hadn't seen Xelloss since dinner the night before. Maybe I had the faint inkling that going after Raltaak was why he hadn't been in his room that morning and why he'd seemingly left our party without so much as a parting smile.

But I couldn't say all that. Everyone knew Raltaak was a Mazoku, so they'd figure out that Xelloss was a Mazoku. And I was trying to keep that secret, dammit!

Luckily for me, Xelloss was a fickle guy. When I declared that morning that we could leave without him because he'd show up eventually, everyone believed me.

Well . . . almost everybody. Amelia was fine with it, Gourry was distracted by something shiny, but Zelgadiss, unsurprisingly, didn't buy a word.

He took another long, stony (excuse the pun) look at me. "Are you hiding something?" he asked lowly.

"Hiding what?" I replied with completely believable innocence.

Zel glowered for a minute but eventually gave up. He turned his eyes back to the road and murmured something about "not liking it."

*Stupid Zelgadiss and his stupid healthy skepticism.*

Zel's suspicions only confirmed what I already suspected—that I couldn't hide Xelloss' demonic roots for much longer. Gourry may be an idiot and Amelia may be easily distracted—but as a whole, my party could be pretty good at picking up hints.

I wondered what Zel would do when he found out. I frowned at the thought; Zel had never gotten along with Xelloss, so the revelation could get messy. I doubted they'd fight—Zel's not dumb enough to take on someone as powerful as Xelloss—but I also figured that Zel might storm off and never talk to us again.

It wasn't like he was traveling with me for his health, anyway—he just wanted to become a human again, after a certain someone turned him into a chimera made of golem and blow demon. Since typical magic couldn't fix him, his last hope was straight out of myth and legend, and that's where I tend to tread. Any bonding we may've done during a particularly famous incident didn't keep him by my side more than his desire to get what he needed. He'd be gone if the situation got too rocky. (Sorry, I couldn't help myself.)

That left me with one option to keep my team from imploding: find out the truth. Why were Raltaak and his friends trying to kill me? Why was Xelloss trying to save me? I couldn't make any moves until I knew everyone's motives.

*Then* I'd have to do something big. I needed an ace in the hole, something menacing and significant to use as insurance. Whatever Mazoku politics were afoot, I needed something to defend me when the truth came out.

*And I know exactly where to start looking.* I glanced up from my boots. The highway stretched out in front of me, as promising as a finger pointed in the direction of loot.

*To Galia, the Sleeping City!*

★★★

Galia was packed, even in the afternoon. People milled around the booths that crowded the busy streets; the overlapping noises of chatting and clomping boots were only broken up by the occasional screaming kid. The city was both big and booming—something to be expected of the capitol of Dilse.

Less expected were the soldiers. They didn't exactly blend into the crowd that bustled around them.

I turned to my party and flashed them a determined look. Amelia nodded and responded with a determined fist clench.

I'd been pretty clever about my intentions, by the way. I'd said I was there to find out what Mazoku were after me and why, since Galia was known for its demonic legends. And all that extra secret information I had? Still secret, thank you very much.

We'd arrived just before noon to grab an inn and a quick bite. Now that we were settled, it was time to nab some info.

"Where do we start?" Amelia asked as her eyes ran down busy Main Street. "If we want to know what the demons are up to, I doubt we'll find rumors about what they're planning in the middle of a city."

"You may be right, Amelia." I mulled over that one for a second. "Hm . . . okay, then how about this? We'll start off simple—get a hold of any rumors you can about any demons in general."

Zel looked dubious. "You can't get any more specific?" he asked.

"Just hear me out, all right?" I emphasized my evolving argument by jabbing a finger in the air. "The word from guards in the Kataart Mountain Range is that the Mazoku are looking for something. Since there used to be a manuscript here, there may be something left over from that. That means we're going through tales at the Sorcerers' Guild.

"Not that we'll figure out the Mazoku plan in one go," I added, "but we might get a lead, or even some insurance for the next time those demons show their ugly mugs." I shrugged. "I know it's a long shot, but we're out of options. We can't just wait for them to show up and try to kill me again, can we?"

*Particularly since Xelloss isn't here,* I didn't add.

Which brings me to my *actual* plan. Before we'd lost him, Xelloss had agreed to travel with us—but his real goal still seemed to be protecting me and taking me with him to the Claire Bible. And yes, I mean the mystic tomes of legend full of otherworldly sorcery techniques. Maybe the general populace thought they were myths, but I don't have much in common with the general populace.

I didn't know *why* Xelloss wanted to bring me to the Claire Bible, but I also knew that I couldn't ask him directly where the thing was. If he just waltzed to the end of the planet and pointed out a tome most people didn't think existed, Zelgadiss and the others would be whining things like "How'd he do that?!" and "What is he?!" until my brain turned to pudding.

That was why I was using Galia as a cover. If I sent everyone off to gather information and Xelloss happened to show up later with mysterious info of his own, everyone could assume he got it from Galia. No questions, no whining, no mess.

Even better, I had my own business in Galia. The stuff I mentioned to Zel about looking for insurance was true—I wanted my trump card for when the Mazoku plans got out. I'd found a lead to a "forbidden spell" in Galia once upon a time, a tale related to the Lord of Nightmares. And based on Xelloss' behavior, I figured that there really *was* a trump card useable against him in the region.

It was worth a shot, anyway.

I quickly scanned my memory before I split off from the group. What else could I remember about Galia? When a certain gorgeous country girl and the snotty, perplexing female she was traveling with for no good reason entered Galia years before, they'd heard some interesting things at the Royal Palace. Hadn't they?

"Amelia," I said. "Do you know the royals here? I was hoping you could pick their brains."

Amelia thought on that one for a second. Since Amelia's of royal blood from the Holy Kingdom of Saillune, I like to use her connections now and then. Too bad that doesn't always come through because her family situation is weird as hell.

"Well," she offered at last, "I think Father knows someone here, but I doubt anyone will recognize me. Galia's pretty far from home."

I folded my arms. *So much for that.*

"Then can you ask around at the temple?" I asked. "Tell them you're researching demon legends from country to country."

She nodded. "Got it."

"Zel." I turned to him. "I want you to get information from around the city. Stop in as many places as you can."

He shrugged. "It's not like I have any other options," he muttered.

"I'll go poke around at the Sorcerers' Guild myself. That leaves . . ." I trailed off as my eyes moved to Gourry. As usual, he was plowing ahead in silence, probably not listening to a word I said.

Gourry cuts a pretty impressive figure: tall, built, and reasonably attractive. Not even my old sword instructor could've won against Gourry in a sword fight, considering Gourry had become an unstoppable swordsmanship *beast* as of late. It was just his brain that was the problem. Or rather, his lack thereof.

I knew that asking Gourry to do reconnaissance was a waste of time, considering the guy could barely touch his left and right feet with his left and right hands. Sending him off on his own was akin to sending him off a cliff.

"Gourry," I said. "Go with Zel."

He glanced back (and down) at me. "Okay."

I gestured to the white shroud over Zel's face. "Since Zel isn't taking that off inside the city, it'll put people on their guard. We need somebody less threatening."

Zelgadiss nodded knowingly.

"And I can't send Gourry alone because he's an idiot," I added.

Gourry nodded knowingly.

I resisted the urge to smack the guy's empty head.

"Work as a team," I told them. "Zel's got the sharp tongue, but Gourry's got the friendly face. Zel can do the talking, and Gourry can just . . . turn to the side and flap his lips, I guess, so it looks like Zel's words are coming out of his mouth." I stopped at the end of my statement, a little stunned by my own genius. That was one of the best plans I'd come up with yet!

Gourry stared at me, confused. "Then I'm gonna be a dummy?" he asked.

*In more ways than one.*

"Ventriloquism," Amelia said thoughtfully. "I never thought of that. Although the whole thing would look pretty bizarre if anyone noticed Zel's lips moving, too."

"Leave the details to the boys." I waved a hand dismissively. "We'll meet back at the inn for dinner, okay?" I started off in my own direction down the street, but Gourry's voice stopped me.

"Lina." He frowned. "Are you sure about this?"

I sighed. Another complaint? Half of my elaborate plans were specifically made to avoid annoying questions!

"What?" I asked thinly.

"Well . . . it feels like every time I look lately, more demons are after you." He scratched the back of his neck. "Should you be really going around by yourself?"

Amelia, Zel, and I all stared at Gourry in shock. He looked uncomfortable under our gaze and shuffled his feet.

"Mister Gourry!" Amelia cried. "You just formulated a reasonable opinion and voiced a concern!"

"And it wasn't about food or why your shoes are on the wrong feet, either." I whistled. "It's been a while since you've participated. Is your brain finally scraping itself together from a swamp of sludge into a hearty ball of muck?"

"It would be nice if you did that more often," Zel added.

They were supposed to be compliments, kinda, but they didn't come out right. Gourry looked like he wasn't sure if he was in trouble or not.

I quickly came up with a reason to simultaneously ease his tiny mind and get him off my back. "I'll be fine," I assured him. "Up until now, the demons have only attacked at night. They may be trying to avoid dragging citizens into this, although . . . hm." I paused. "They *did* attack me at the inn, but that only ended up luring me away. That still mostly fits the 'no innocents involved' theory.

"Whatever the case, I'm pretty sure they want to take me out when I'm alone. I doubt they'll attack in a city full of people."

"Oh." Gourry still looked worried. "Um . . . I guess?"

"Relax, Gourry." I flashed him a confident smile. "If I was paranoid about this, I couldn't even go to the bathroom alone. And who wants that, really?"

As Gourry seemed to mull that over, I secretly ground my teeth. I *did not* want him coming with me to the Sorcerers' Guild. He'd done that once before and gotten me kicked out because of his whining and arguing. All I'd done was smack him with a book when he'd fallen asleep in the library—it's not my fault those Guilds carry five-hundred page tomes with gold-reinforced hard covers. I wasn't going through that embarrassment again.

"Anyway," I called, taking off briskly down the street so it wouldn't be easy to stop me. "Follow the plan, everybody. See you at dinner."

I peeked behind me a second later. The other members of my party had started heading off, but they didn't look happy about it.

***

I was stepping around a curve in the road, my mind elsewhere, when a useful bit of info suddenly hit me.

Literally.

"Ack!" A small boy ran into me at full speed, nearly knocking me off my feet. I deftly took a few steps to regain my balance as the boy swung an arm in desperate circles to do the same.

"Hey," I snapped as I untangled my mantle. "What's your hurry, pipsqueak?"

The boy mumbled a rushed apology. He looked eleven or twelve; had wavy, glossy black hair; and looked kinda like a girl. He shot off ahead of me, but I rushed forward and grabbed him by the back of the shirt before he could get far.

The boy looked up fearfully. "Wh-what do you want?!" he demanded.

I gave a sarcastic chuckle. "My purse," I answered.

"The one you just stole. Unless you'd rather I called a soldier?" I gave him an evil smile, all teeth.

The boy went pale. He hurriedly pulled my purse of gold coins out of a pocket.

"Here!" he cried as he shoved it into my hands. "Just . . . just take it and let me go! I don't even care if you beat me up—just don't hand me over to those psychos!"

I raised an eyebrow. "Psychos?" I repeated. That wasn't a word I normally associated with city guards, no matter how annoying they could be.

"Yeah," the boy confirmed, his body visibly shaking now. "The guards around here have all been really weird lately!"

*Interesting.* I could tell the little pickpocket was my ticket to Informationville. And since he was nervous, I could take advantage.

"I'll tell you what," I said at last, making sure to keep my grip on his shirt. "I'll let this little incident slide if you come with me. I want to hear more about these guards."

He looked up with big eyes. "Come with you where?" he asked.

★★★

I brought the girly little boy to a restaurant. It wasn't until his orange juice had arrived and he'd sniveled into it for a while that he started with the good stuff.

"The soldiers here are crazy," he whined. "And so's the king."

"And?" I didn't tell him to man up because I was afraid he'd burst into tears. "Can you be any more specific?"

He rubbed his eyes with the back of a hand. "The king's been hiring a whole bunch of troops and traveling sorcerers lately," he explained.

My eyes shot open. "What?!" I cried.

My voice was so loud that the boy looked up at me in terror.

I grimaced and glanced around, but it looked like none of the few other customers in there cared about our conversation.

I cleared my throat and said in a harsh whisper, "You mean the king's preparing for war?!"

The boy squirmed in his seat and swallowed hard. "I dunno," he mumbled. "It's been a few years since the king first started ordering more troops, but now I think there're more sorcerers than warriors. And people say they're teaching black magic to the regular troops."

"Black magic?!" I hissed, just barely remembering to keep my voice down. "You'd better be kidding!"

The boy shrunk back in his chair as his eyes brimmed with tears. When he started to sniffle, I threw myself back into my own chair and angrily crossed my arms. The kid needed at least another minute to freak out before he'd talk to me again.

My mind raced. I mean, yeah, sure, I understood teaching some offensive magic to soldiers. It would make them better at their job, right? But why black magic? Who in their right mind thought *that* was a good idea?!

Let's say I'm a sorcerer drill sergeant or something. If all the foot soldiers I'm training have no prior knowledge of sorcery, I'm going to teach them a simple fire spell— something like Flare Arrow. It's popular and really common, but that's because it's *extremely practical* in combat. It's one the easiest offensive spells to teach; it's plenty good against human opponents; and you can use to it set fire to, say, enemy headquarters.

I don't think I'd teach black magic by design *or* accident. Black magic may have more offensive power than an elemental Flare Arrow spell and do damage to demons and non-corporal undead like ghosts, but it's hard to teach and usually has no practical side effects (like setting things on fire). And if you aren't doing the proper body motions necessary to control the spell while casting it, all hell breaks loose.

Black magic's too complex to teach to bottom-of-the-barrel *sorcerers,* let alone non-sorcerers. You'd think the term "black magic" would evoke fear in people—or at least respect. But apparently there were dingbats out there who thought it was a cool blasty power to put into the hands of soldier flunkies. *Ugh,* I thought. *People are idiots.*

The boy had finally gotten over his sniffing and was looking into his juice.

"Are you sure about the black magic?" I asked him. "Who'd you hear this from?"

The boy took a tentative sip. "I've never seen it myself or anything," he mumbled, "but that's what the rumors say. They say the king's gotten weird since General Rashatt arrived. They say they're using dragons and elves and stuff now."

"Dragons and elves?" I repeated.

The boy shrugged. "There's a big elf village west of the city, and to the north there's Dragon's Peak in the Kataart Mountains. So they come from there, I guess."

I was starting to understand why the boy used terms like *weird* and *psycho;* the whole situation was completely bizarre. Even if a kingdom *was* preparing to wage war, dragons and elves wouldn't help humans no matter how much they—

My thoughts stopped abruptly. "No way!" I shouted as I jumped to my feet.

The boy hadn't yet flashed me his warning look before I remembered I was supposed to be quiet. A quick check around the room reminded me, once more, that nobody in the place gave a crap about me.

"What's the matter?" the boy asked.

"Nothing," I said through gritted teeth, trying to sound as calm as possible despite the cold sweat running down my back. If my worst-case-scenario hunch was right . . .

It sounded like the country was picking a fight with the demons in the Kataart Mountains.

"They're picking a fight with the Kataart Mountains?!" Amelia, stealthily seated at a nearby table, suddenly jumped out of her chair in an overload of Love and Justice.

*That* was when every single customer in the restaurant—and the waitress, the proprietor, and some guy who stuck his head out of the kitchen—all stared at us like we were circus freaks. A small chorus of indignant mumbling started up.

I whipped around to her. "Amelia!" I whisper-shouted. "What are you doing here?! And keep it down!"

Amelia didn't seem bothered by angry customers in the slightest. "We don't have time for social niceties!" she announced loudly as she marched to my table. "The foul hands of demons may be about to fall on this city!"

"The key word is *may*," I hissed. "This is all guesswork based on rumor, okay? So save your heroics and screaming for when we actually know what's going on!"

Amelia hesitated, a thoughtful frown tugging at her lips. "Well . . . you may be right," she said with obvious skepticism. She let out a breath and plopped down in a free chair.

The boy took one look at her, then stared at me incredulously. "Is she with you?" he asked in a rude tone.

"Yes," I said through my teeth. "And you're not. Scram."

The boy seemed relieved to finally be free of me. He raced out of the restaurant, but I kept my hand in my pocket to touch my money purse until he vanished.

***

As planned, Amelia and I met up with the boys that night. We assembled around a dinner table to discuss our information over grub.

Unfortunately, mentioning my theory about the country attacking demons set Amelia off again. We lost several minutes and a few pieces of dishware before we could calm her down enough for us to discuss everything like sane people.

"I think it's true that the king's assembling troops and sorcerers," Zelgadiss said as he brushed away some stray food that had landed on his shoulder during Amelia's freak-out.

"Did you pick that up when asking around?" I asked.

He nodded. "It's a pretty significant number of troops, apparently. But other than that, are you sure about all that talk of black magic and elves and dragons? It was only a kid telling you this."

I sighed. "Who knows if it's true? But using the term *black magic* seems a little specific for some kid spinning lies to mess with me."

Amelia clenched her fist. "If it's a dangerous issue that an adult would avoid talking about, then only hearing it from a child makes perfect sense!" she declared with completely meaningless zeal. She pointed at me dramatically. "Lina! Do you know where that child went? We should speak to him again!"

"Well . . . he was just some passing street kid," I replied. "I'm pretty sure he didn't even say his name."

I avoided mentioning that he'd introduced himself by grabbing my purse. If I said that, Amelia would start a rant about how he deserved some Justice right in the kisser.

"So we really have no idea if anything he said is true," Zel said flatly.

"Then we should find out for certain!" Amelia speared a fried shrimp ball with her fork for emphasis. "At the very least we have to discover that there's no threat before we can relax!"

In a way, I did agree with her. The potential for disaster was huge.

"Although a subjugation of demons in itself could be a good thing," she continued, "and although such an action would require commendable bravery, it's too reckless a decision. Especially if it's conducted by a general of dubious origin!"

"Who could be out of his melon," I added.

Gourry dug his fork into a potato. "Is it really that crazy of a plan if he has dragons and elves helping?" he asked.

"Yes," I answered flatly.

"Why?" He asked so vaguely that it almost sounded like he was arguing with himself.

I leaned back in my chair. "Elves and dragons are definitely more powerful on average than humans, but demons are in their own league. Legend says that when Ruby Eye descended into the Kataart Mountains during the Demon War a millennium ago, a single demon defeated several *hundred* dragons there." I spun my spoon in my fingers. "Even accounting for the exaggeration of myth, demons are way more badass than dragons.

"If a bunch of humans bring elves and dragons to their demon fight, at best they'll kick up more dirt. It's still a stupid idea."

"Huh." Gourry tilted his head a little. "Then . . . why would the king do something so dumb?"

"That's what we're trying to figure *out,* Gourry."

"It's possible," Zel said evenly, "that the king wants to avenge his father."

I pondered that a second. It *was* a possibility.

The country's previous king—Dilus II, Dilus Luon Galia, also known as the Resolute King—had raised an army to subjugate the demons of the Kataart Mountains twenty years earlier. At the end, he personally led five thousand crack troops with a core force of sorcerers across Dragon's Peak; they headed north into the mountains, only to vanish from history. All that remained of the team were rumors . . . and a general fear of the power of Kataart.

The current king—Dilus III, Dilus Kuolto Galia— probably knew that better than anyone, but maybe his twenty-year-old anger had finally hit the boiling point? *Anger can make you nuts,* I thought, remembering some of the things I've done while pissed. Unless somebody had just put the idea in his head and was egging him on.

Amelia's cry broke off my thoughts. "We have to look into this!" she screeched, adding nothing new to our discussion. "Maybe . . . yes! This General Rashatt in particular is highly suspicious! If he slipped into the country and began scheming and taking advantage of people, we can never forgive him!"

"We don't know if he's guilty of anything yet," I pointed out.

She didn't stop to breathe. "But we have to act quickly if he *is* behind this! We'll uncover the truth with our own hands!"

I was starting to guess why Amelia was acting even more justice-crazed than usual. A while back, Saillune had its Royal Palace infiltrated by a demon, which resulted in a pretty serious fanning of the family feud's flames. A stranger suddenly appearing at the palace, an atmosphere of national unrest . . . Dilse was probably looking an awful lot like Saillune right now.

Amelia stared at me, her eyes blazing. "You'll all help out, won't you?!"

I shrunk back in my chair a little. The gist of the situation was clear, but the details were getting more and more tangled by the minute.

*We need a better plan,* I wanted to say, but in her state, I doubted she'd hear me. *This sounds like a giant pain in the ass* was another thought, but I knew that one wouldn't get me very far.

"Fine," I muttered at last.

Amelia made some sort of victorious snort and whipped her head to Zelgadiss.

Zel shrugged. "There's no reason for me to refuse."

"If Mister Zelgadiss agrees," Amelia said triumphantly, "that only leaves Mister Gourry. And since he doesn't really contemplate, a nod is more than enough."

Gourry nodded, then slurped his soup.

I refrained from commenting, *This is why people don't respect you, Gourry.*

"All right!" Amelia slammed a fist on the table. "Now we can do this!"

I snatched a piece of bread. "We should probably confirm those rumors first, then."

She slammed the table again, this time knocking over Zel's tea. "You're too soft, Lina!" she roared. "The blood in my veins tells me there's a *conspiracy* afoot! We don't have time to confirm rumors—we have to go straight to finding direct evidence of the conspiracy!"

"Um . . ." I raised an eyebrow. "And how exactly do we do that? If the conspiracy's unfolding at the Royal Palace, we'd probably have to go there, meet the general face to face, and get him to talk." I pointed at her with my knife. "But since you yourself said no one knows you there, we won't get past the front gate."

Amelia folded her arms and looked up at the ceiling in thought.

Gourry suddenly chimed in with a stupid plan.

"Hey, guys!" he said. "How about we make some trouble and get arrested? We'd probably get to meet the general that way."

*Sigh.*

"Gourry," I said flatly, "generals don't come to visit common criminals."

Gourry didn't seem convinced. "But, I mean . . ."

"You mean what?" I leveled a stare at him.

Amelia nodded enthusiastically. "I think Mister Gourry may be right!" she declared. "Once we're arrested, we can quietly break out of jail and go get our proof!"

I was sorely tempted to drop my face into my soup. I took a deep breath.

"Listen," I said slowly and very clearly. "Assuming we do that, and assuming we find the best damn proof ever, who's gonna believe it coming from a bunch of crooks? We'll be felons at that point," I added; I couldn't make any assumptions with that crowd.

Amelia paused, then clapped her hands together in front of her chest.

"Justice always wins," she recited. "If we find our proof, we'll make it work somehow!"

"*If* we find our proof!" I snapped. "I already said we're going off rumor. What if we get arrested, break out, *and* find the general, and all this mess turns out to be nothing?"

"But . . . Mister Zelgadiss said they really are gathering soldiers and sorcerers!" she retorted.

"It could easily be a domestic dispute or some new training for the army. Even if the dragons and elves thing is true, they may just want to defend themselves if the demons of Kataart attack *them*." I sighed. "We're worried about this country *invading* Kataart. If it's anything else, it's a local issue and not our problem.

"Which brings me to my original point: We need to confirm the rumors before we do anything drastic. We'll worry about using proof to stop the general from manipulating the king into a suicidal war *after* we find out whether or not that's actually happening."

I had everyone's attention at last. Well . . . in a way. Amelia had shut up, Zelgadiss was brooding, and Gourry was licking his plate.

"I know how we can do this," I said. "If they're using dragons and elves, they need people who speak Dragon and Elvish. If they're teaching soldiers black magic, they obviously need sorcerers. The Sorcerers' Guild would know if those sorts of people were being gathered. We'll go there first, then try the city's information brokers."

Amelia finally seemed to like my not-insane plan. "Good!" she cried as she jumped to her feet. "So Mister Zelgadiss and Mister Gourry will ask around the city, and you and I will go to the Sorcerer's Guild!"

. . . I hadn't counted on being stuck with Amelia through all this. She was going to be insufferable, wasn't she?

I sighed. *Oh, well,* I thought as I pushed back my chair. *It still beats bringing Gourry.*

***

Two days later, as I sat in the library of the Sorcerers' Guild, a prediction of mine came true.

"Lina Inverse, I presume," came a voice from above.

I looked up. A soldier in full armor towered over my table; a small cluster of other soldiers armed similarly were flanking him. The armed unit looked pretty out of place in a room full of books. I noticed all the other sorcerers in the library staring at us.

*Here we go.* "I think you've got the wrong girl," I said casually. I never play it straight when ambushed—it's better to try and trick your opponent so you can make some kind of getaway.

The soldier wasn't at all phased by my You've-Got-The-Wrong-Girl Attack. "Lina Inverse, I presume," he repeated without blinking an eye.

*Stiffs. Great.* But as I mentioned, I sorta expected this. Amelia and I had split our duties at the Sorcerers' Guild— she asked around while I hit the history books—so I was spending most of my time alone. I'd decided to skimp on the reading of recent national history and instead looked up old legends for a clue on how to fight demons.

Anyway, the real cincher was that I didn't have to register when I came into the library. That probably meant somebody was expecting me.

"That's me," I admitted at last, closing my book with a *thump.*

"If you would come with us to the castle."

*Figures.* Their armor was the kind formally worn by Royal Knights. What I hadn't yet figured out was *why* I was being asked to the palace for some sort of . . . chat. Or beating, maybe.

"Why?" I asked, deciding to be direct.

"We know nothing beyond the facts that you would be here and we must bring you," the knight replied in an intensely serious tone.

He was making my wiggling out of this very difficult. If he'd said "I can't say," I could've shot back with, "I can't respond to a summons if you won't tell me what it's for." But now, if I accused his *order* of being suspicious and caused a ruckus, I'd just look like I had something to hide. I didn't have a choice but to play along.

"Fine," I said after a second. "Just let me tell the girl I'm with first—she'll worry if I disappear on her."

The soldier paused. "Make it quick," he said curtly.

I returned my book to its shelf, exited the library, and started looking around for Amelia. The soldiers followed at my heels, making us all look like we were playing a game of Follow The Leader for Stupid Adults.

Because I was about as conspicuous wandering around as a roast pig on a vegetarian platter, Amelia found me first.

"Lina!" she cried as she ran up. She took one look at me, then at the soldiers, then back at me.

"What did you do *now?!*" she shrieked loud enough for half the city to hear.

"Keep it down!" I snapped. "I have a reputation!" I jerked a thumb at the brain brigade behind me. "They want me to go to the palace with them."

Amelia raised her eyebrows. "Are you sure that's safe?" she asked in a barely quiet whisper. "Maybe I should go with you."

I waved a hand dismissively. "I'll be fine. If something bad happens, I'll just blow the place up and meet you back at the Guild."

Since I made sure to say that last part loud enough to be heard, one of the knights made a surprised and angry snort.

"But that's only if I'm put in danger," I added. "If I'm just being brought there to talk, I wouldn't *dream* of being difficult."

The same knight made another snort, this one more subdued. I was pretty sure the soldiers understood what I was implying.

"Tell the others, Amelia." I turned to the knights. "We can get going now."

As I walked off with my own personal guard unit, I pretended not to notice the worried look on Amelia's face.

***

Beyond the palace gates lay a vast green lawn. A white stone path cut through the brilliant green and ended at the dark-stoned, austere Royal Palace.

The building wasn't fancy, but it definitely looked sturdy. The palace and its surrounding area was enclosed by a stone wall; isolated buildings dotted the compound here and there. In front of one of the non-castle buildings was some important-looking guy—Captain of the Guard, probably—giving instructions to a line of knights.

"This way."

The knights led me to a building on the right a little ways away. The place was flanked by several other soldiers.

. . . I knew this pattern. Somebody was going to attack me by surprise. I clenched my fists and kept walking as casually as possible.

One of the knights walked to the door and shouted at it, "We've brought Lina Inverse!"

"Enter!" a gatekeeper yelled back.

The knight opened the door and led us through. The room inside was pretty big—it looked like some kind of conference area, maybe. A trio of men sat around a large table in the center of the room.

One looked like a sorcerer. He was middle-aged and seemed eccentric, which was part of what tipped me off. The other two were soldiers: one older and Spartan, the other younger and handsome.

The middle-aged soldier rose to his feet and smiled. "So you're Miss Lina Inverse," he said in a surprisingly friendly tone. "We've heard so much—it's an honor to meet you. Forgive us for summoning you here so suddenly."

I stopped for a second, confused. The greeting wasn't exactly what I expected.

*Um . . . nobody's trying to kill me,* I thought. *Why is nobody trying to kill me?*

"I am Rashatt," he went on. "General of Dilse's armed forces."

"Huh?!" The instant I blurted my shock, I regretted it. Rashatt was obviously taken aback by my outburst.

I was just surprised, all right? So sue me!

*Keep it together, Lina!*

"Is it something about my name?" Rashatt offered carefully.

I quickly shook my head and threw out my hands. "No!" I exclaimed. "Ah, no. I just heard about you from an old friend. That's all, really."

I couldn't believe it. If Rashatt was the evil mastermind behind the suicidal demon slaughter, why was he being so open and nice?! I practically heard the entire world laughing at me.

Rashatt gestured to the table. "At any rate, Miss Lina—please have a seat. I've summoned you here today because I have a favor to ask of you."

I swallowed and took a chair. Whatever he had to say, I had to pretend he wasn't freaking me out.

He sat down and folded his hands together. "I think this needs no explanation," he began, "but to the north of this nation lie the Kataart Mountains, a dwelling of demons. This country has been threatened by that menace since its founding.

"It's important to note that demons have not *yet* launched a full-scale invasion," he admitted, "but there's no guarantee that they won't one day do so. If that were to happen, our means of resistance would be rather meager."

*Okay, then.*

As I sat back and listened to his piece, a soldier brought some drinks over. I passed; there was no guarantee Rashatt wasn't being nice just to lower my guard and drug me.

"The best we have is a small fort near Kataart where soldiers are stationed to observe the mountains. However, while this can keep unwary humans from going to Kataart, it will be of little use if demons descend. These men could do no more than send a panicked messenger to raise a call to arms; slowing a demon advancement is beyond them."

Rashatt glanced in the direction of the middle-aged sorcerer. "We've been teaching offensive magic to our soldiers to improve our chance of resistance. We asked Galia's Sorcerers' Guild for assistance, and I hoped for Vice-Chairman to personally give instruction . . . but it's proven to be difficult for those without the relevant experience to understand how offensive magic is to be used in actual battle.

"As luck would have it, the librarian at the Guild library recognized you. And I've heard rumors that you are experienced in fighting demons." He leaned forward a bit, his gaze intent.

"Lina Inverse . . . would you be interested in teaching offensive combat magic to our soldiers?"

My mouth opened, but it took me a second to make any sound. "Hm," I managed at last, leaning back in my chair. I folded my arms and took a deep breath.

Well, so much for me preparing for the worse. I'd pretty much put money on General Rashatt greeting me alone, revealing the fact that he was a Mazoku, laughing maniacally while rambling off anywhere from ten to one hundred percent of the demons' scheme, and then getting pounded when Gourry and the others arrived for no good reason.

It had made sense in my head. And honestly, that's how a fair chunk of our adventures work out. "This wasn't what I was expecting," I murmured.

Rashatt heard me, apparently. "What *did* you expect?" he asked.

I quickly covered. "Oh, you know," I said in a brush-off manner. "I didn't expect all *this*. You know."

When he just stared at me, I made stuff up as fast as I could. "I'm just . . . it's not that I have an urgent trip tomorrow morning or anything, but I am pretty busy. And I don't intend to stay in Galia for very long, anyway. Oh—and I have people traveling with me. You know how that can be."

"Ah," Rashatt said, quickly waving his hands. "I have no intention to keep you long. A month, perhaps, or ten days? Even two or three days is fine if that's all you can spare." He nodded knowingly. "Of course, I realize that it would be unreasonable to ask you to teach magic in such a short time, so I would be more than grateful if you just passed on tips: when to use combat spells, what to watch out for, how demons fight, and so on."

I thought on that one for a minute. If General Rashatt *was* some kind of demon, he could be laying a trap. What better way to catch me by surprise than by keeping me locked in the castle with a job?

On the other hand, if the general was just a regular guy and everything he'd said was on the level, his proposition sounded annoying at worst. Annoying I could deal with—especially for a few days. I was used to dealing with annoying.

Whatever I decided, I had to tell the others. Amelia would probably assume our worst fears were true and knock down the castle gates if I didn't meet up with her soon.

"Look," I said at last. "I'll think it over. I need to go back and discuss it with my companions in the city."

"That would be problematic," Rashatt replied.

I raised an eyebrow. "Really," I said carefully. "And why is that?"

"This matter is still being kept secret from the public," the general replied calmly. "Despite the fact that our plan is one of defense, it may appear to others that we're preparing for war with other nations. I wish to avoid having needless misunderstandings arise."

I couldn't argue that. I'd assumed something far more dangerous and sinister than "defense" myself.

"We intend to make this public once all preparations and arrangements have been completed. I would ask that you speak to no one of this." Rashatt paused. "If your companions can keep this secret, as well, I don't mind your speaking with them, but doing so in the city would be problematic."

I shrugged. "Then do you mind calling them here? I'll wait while messengers bring them in from the city."

Rashatt stroked his chin. "In that case . . ."

***

The room they gave me was less than lavish.

It was isolated—predictably—and had a single bed, a table cut out of black oak, and two matching chairs. A pitcher rested on top of the table.

*Whatever,* I thought. The place wasn't fancy, but it passed. I had more important things on my mind.

The soldier who had led me there still stood in the doorway. "Please wait here," he said evenly. "I'll summon your companions." He closed the door and walked down the hallway, but I waited until the sound of his steps faded before I finally relaxed.

"Phew." I flopped onto the bed, which turned out to be comfortable. I rolled onto my back and stared at the ceiling.

I was still pretty confused about the whole situation, so I lay there for a while to think. I worked through a number of possible situations that ended in my dying, my *not* dying, and plenty of things in-between. I'd nearly made myself dizzy with the possibilities when the sound of more footsteps broke my thoughts.

I quickly sat up. It was too early to be Gourry and everyone. *So who is it?* I wondered.

Finally, the footsteps came to a halt just outside my room.

*Click.* A small metallic sound made my heart drop to my stomach. I jumped to my feet.

Someone had just locked me in.

"Heh heh," chuckled a disembodied voice I'd never heard before. "This is the end for you, Lina Inverse."

I finished casting a wind barrier and ducked under the oak table.

BOOOOOOM! The stone wall next to my door suddenly exploded. The force of whatever had blasted it made my room shake, sending dust and pebbles spewing in at me. I ducked my head under my arms.

"What the hell?!" I cried as I coughed.

It took a few seconds for the echo of the explosion to trail off. As I tried to hack the dust out of my lungs, I thanked my lucky stars for an idiot attacker—I'd managed to cast and complete that wind barrier while he'd dramatically turned the key and declared victory.

*Hubris,* I thought. *How many times have you saved my butt?*

I spit the last of the dust from my mouth and stood. I peered into the darkness, but I couldn't see anybody.

. . . So I *was* in a trap. The good news was that I wasn't dead. The bad news was that whoever had been outside my door hadn't cast a spell—his attack had come directly after him saying he would kill me. There was only one kind of creature that could activate a spell without casting it.

A Mazoku.

I fleetingly wondered if that meant General Rashatt *was* a demon, but more immediate thoughts of survival took priority. The blast had blown through my wall and the wall opposite it, which led outside. I leapt into the night air and ran as fast I could across the palace lawn.

"Hey!"

"Over there!"

I cursed under my breath as a number of soldiers ran toward me. I couldn't afford to get captured, but I wasn't about to kill flunkies who probably had nothing to do with this. I hurriedly chanted a spell for flight.

"You're still alive?" someone hissed hatefully from above.

I jerked my head up. A single silhouette floated in the air. I ground my teeth together. The thing wasn't a person, obviously, even though its size and general shape were humanoid. The thing's twisting, convulsing body was charcoal black, its face was snow white, and its extremely wide-set eyes were red as blood.

For a second, I wondered if it was General Rashatt in his true form, but his voice was different. This demon's voice was definitely the one I'd heard outside my room.

Of course, demons more powerful than my new floating friend could disguise themselves as completely believable humans. He might be able to swing changing the tone and pitch of his voice . . .

*Forget it, Lina!* I reminded myself angrily. *Worry about it after you get back to your teammates in one piece!*

"This time," the demon snarled, "I'll show no mercy!"

The moment he spoke, countless pale-blue balls of light popped up around him and started shooting off in all directions.

"Aaagh!" I cut off my thoughts and picked up speed.

BOOM!

One of the balls exploded right behind me. I could barely evade the things as I made a beeline for the palace gates.

"You can't run!" the demon shouted as he shot another ball of light. The ball bore into the ground, smashed into the royal compound's wall, and threw uninvolved soldiers into the air like rag dolls.

He wasn't just firing his power at me—he was shooting it off in all directions. The Royal Palace was taking some serious damage.

*Bastard!* I thought. Some demons have scruples when they fight, but this guy was a real ass.

I managed to evade the demon's attacks by zig-zagging across the lawn. After I jumped through the hole he'd smashed in the lawn's wall, I ventured a quick glance over my shoulder.

He was still chasing me. In fact, the guy looked ready to tear down the world.

"I said you can't run!" he shouted as more balls of light sprang up around him.

I couldn't believe what I was seeing. "Don't!" I screamed, screeching to a halt without thinking. I was already dozens of steps into the city.

Whether or not he heard me didn't seem to matter— the next instant he'd turned Galia into a sea of flames.

# 2: TOWARD THE LEGENDARY PEAK OF THE DRAGONS

Fire surged through Galia, bathing the night a terrifying orange. The roaring of flames and the screaming of fleeing citizens mingled in my ears.

But he still didn't stop. As I stood there in shock, my eyes fixed on the engulfing flames, I heard the demon's explosions continue from somewhere nearby. His form was concealed by the flames and smoke.

The demon had attacked the entire area with little distinction. I knew he was only after me, but he was taking down a *city* to do it. Was he destroying my surroundings so I didn't have anywhere to run? Or was this the only way he could use his power?

Whatever his motivation, I couldn't just stand there. I clenched my fist.

I had to lure him out of the city.

It wasn't too keen on being bait, obviously, but I didn't have a choice. I wouldn't be able to sleep for who knew how long if I let all of Galia take a fall for me.

I quickly chanted a high-speed flight spell. I couldn't fire off heavy offensive magic while using it, so against a demon, it was only good for running away. And even with a wind barrier deployed around me, my physical safety was in doubt if I took a direct hit from a major spell.

But disadvantage or no, I couldn't use fancy offensive spells in the middle of a city. And trying to lure the demon away on foot would never work.

*I can already tell this is gonna suck.*

"Ray Wing!" I shouted.

A wind barrier enveloped my body, lifting me into the sky. I burst through the black smoke to find the demon . . . and, after a second, I *did* find a demon. There was just one problem.

It wasn't the same demon.

My jaw dropped. The new demon hovering before me had skin the color of a drowned corpse, and there was a single giant eye in the center of his face.

*Those sons of* . . . I could barely think the swears I meant to throw at them. They were planning to get me with a pincer attack!

The moment the demon noticed me, he fired a black shockwave in my direction. I barely controlled my spell in time to avoid the attack and fly toward the edge of the city.

The first demon appeared in front of me again.

*Dammit!* The situation was getting worse by the second.

The demon formed a pale blue energy lance and fired it at me. I altered the course of my flight.

WHAM!

I let out a strangled cry as shockwaves and heat hit me. The demon behind me had launched another attack!

The hit didn't do any damage since it was blocked by the wind barrier, but it definitely threw my concentration off. By the time I could focus again, the lance of light from the demon in front was zooming straight for me.

My heart practically stopped. It was too late to dodge!

The lance of light easily sliced through my wind barrier and vanished into thin air with a mild buzzing sound.

I stared dumbly at where the lance had vanished. *What the hell?* I wondered as the demon in front moved his gaze to something behind me.

Another silhouette appeared beside the demon who'd thrown the lance. At almost the same moment, the demon shattered into a million pieces.

The remaining silhouette slowly came into focus. A familiar smile was the first thing I saw through the smoke.

Priest Xelloss.

*About damn time,* I thought as the pounding in my ears began to subside. I swallowed hard and reminded myself to breathe.

I vaguely realized that the demon from behind wasn't attacking anymore. Xelloss had probably destroyed that one, too. Annihilating two demons with a single blow each . . .

Xelloss could still surprise me with his power.

He mouthed something and pointed below us. I couldn't hear what he was saying through the wind barrier, but I understood once I looked down.

I gave him a short nod and cut down through the smoke, setting down once again on a flame-enveloped city street. Xelloss landed beside me a moment later.

As I released my barrier, I noticed that I could no longer sense anyone in Galia. It felt like the populace had cleared out entirely.

"Hm," Xelloss hummed, his smile as calm as ever. "It would seem my arrival was somewhat late."

Considering the situation, his unchanging calm was simultaneously soothing and creepy. I sighed and rubbed my eyes. "A little," I mumbled.

"That means the attack on the village was a plot to draw me away from you. But I never suspected that Mister Raltaak would use *himself* as a decoy." Xelloss chuckled, as amused as a kid at a petting zoo.

"I'm sure this is all hilarious to you," I said thinly, "but we still need to get out of here. I'm already practically medium-rare."

Xelloss nodded and kept in step as I quickly walked down the street.

I glanced at him through the smoke. "Did you take Raltaak down?" I asked.

Xelloss gave me a pained smile. "Er . . . no," he admitted. "He beat me quite easily, I'm afraid. Isn't that inconvenient? Ha ha!"

"How can you be laughing at a time like this?!"

Xelloss shrugged. "He's also a Priest, you see. And the same level, if we're comparing rank. But for them to have a base in this city . . ." He shook his head. "The size of this world never ceases to amaze me."

I scowled. "You're not making me feel any better, Xelloss! And can't you use your power to put out this fire? Those guys hit everything to get at me!"

Xelloss flashed me another pained smile. "Water and ice spells are not exactly my . . ."

"Argh!" I slapped a hand to my forehead. "I can't believe you're useless when the entire city's—"

I stopped my ranting short as I noticed a body at the edge of the street. It was small, vaguely male, and definitely not moving. Red stained the rubble beneath his body.

It was the little boy who'd grabbed my purse.

I ran up without thinking. "Hey!" I called as I dropped to my knees beside him. "Are you okay? Can you—?" I touched his bare skin, then yanked my hand back.

The boy's body was already cold. A wave of shock ran through me.

I slowly stood up. Xelloss took his turn to kneel beside the boy.

"No heartbeat," he said.

"I know that," I snapped, my fingers trembling a little. I knew the kid was beyond my help. I did the only thing I could at that point—I said a brief, silent prayer and continued on my way.

I gritted my teeth. *Dammit,* I thought, my palms growing damper. If I didn't put an end to the whole mess—and soon—who else was going to pay for it? I had to do *something*, but the demons were too powerful for me.

Xelloss' voice cut into my thoughts. "Well?" he inquired. "What do you plan to do from here? I have to admit that I'd be against staying in the city."

I knew I couldn't stay; staying in Galia would make more casualties. I only had one choice.

"Let's find the others," I muttered quietly. "We're getting the hell out of here. And if they've already bolted and I can't find them . . ." I paused a second, then took a breath. "I'll go after the Claire Bible by myself."

***

A single streak of light ripped toward me through the wind and flames.

I cursed and barely dodged. At the same moment the magic light shot past me, a figure burst out of the wall of flames.

It was another demon. I'd just turned to face him when Xelloss exploded the demon's head to bits.

I panted and wiped my streaming forehead. How many of those guys were there?! My raw guess was ten, but I'd lost count after the first few. One thing was for sure—there were *too damn many.*

Xelloss and I were still searching the city for Gourry and the others. We couldn't make much progress, considering the number of demon attacks, and the whole thing made me marvel at how many demons had been lurking around Galia.

The attacking demons were each about as powerful as Seigram or Vizeus; they were only dropping like flies because Xelloss was so badass. I was sure he could've dropped them even if they'd all come out at once. I was just along for the ride like a heroine from the old Heroic Sagas.

Xelloss suddenly stopped and wrapped his mantle around me. I raised my eyebrows at him.

KA-BOOOOOOOOM!

A series of exploding lights burst around us, crumbling the walls of buildings and boiling the earth red. I didn't know if it was the blast or the heat causing all the destruction, but I barely felt anything inside Xelloss' cape.

When the lights finally faded, a humanoid shape approached through the rippling heat waves. Whoever it was halted a little ways in front of us.

"So you've recovered," snapped a voice I most definitely recognized. The bastard even had the balls to wear the armor of Dilse.

General Rashatt glared at Xelloss, his eyes filled with quiet anger.

*I knew you were evil!* I thought at him, but I chose to keep my mouth shut. It looked like the guy didn't appreciate Xelloss interfering with his plan to kill me.

"General Rashatt," Xelloss said in an almost friendly tone. "This is the first time we've met in person, isn't it?"

"The first," Rashatt agreed thinly. "And the last." He took a step toward us. "Sir Raltaak said I wasn't to raise a hand against you, but considering the situation . . ."

"One has no choice but to fight, hm?" Xelloss smiled at Rashatt, egging the man on.

Rashatt gripped the sword tighter in his hand. "Of course," he bellowed. "Now we'll see who survives: Priest or General!"

*Yikes.* Rashatt's radiating bloodlust made me quickly pull back. I was a goner if I got caught in even the *backwash* of those guys fighting. I have my pride and all, but it was a logical time to sit on the sidelines.

Rashatt went first. "Gah!" he cried as the blade in his hands radiated velvety light and transformed into a much stranger sword. It took me a second to realize that he'd probably turned a regular sword into a demon-cutting demonic blade.

He could do that?!

"Hah!" Firing a mass of black energy at Xelloss with his free hand, Rashatt charged after the blast with his new sword at the ready. Xelloss, almost surprisingly, didn't dodge.

BWOOM!

Rashatt's energy mass slammed squarely into Xelloss, making black flashes explode and miasma swirl around. I ducked my head under my arms.

I figured that Xelloss had taken the hit because he knew he could. But Rashatt would know that, wouldn't he? That would mean the attack was just to blind Xelloss. I looked up just in time to see Rashatt leap in with his blade among the explosions.

"Perish, Priest!" he roared.

The clang of metal overlapped Rashatt's cry as he disappeared into light and smoke. When the air finally cleared, it revealed Rashatt's sword buried in Xelloss' chest.

I gave a start. *What?!*

But I was wrong. The sword simply *ended* at Xelloss' chest; with a small but heavy *clunk,* the broken tip of Rashatt's sword buried itself in the ground by my feet. It dissolved in the wind, retaking the shape of the original sword for a moment, then dissolved again to leave a small mass of silvery metal on the ground.

Somehow, Xelloss had broken Rashatt's blade before it could hit him. Rashatt looked both dazed and a little frightened as he stumbled backward.

Xelloss, injury-free, smiled his disturbing little smile at Rashatt. "Shall I teach you?" he asked lightly. "Would you like to know why Mister Raltaak told you not to raise your hand against me?"

Before he'd even finished talking, a corkscrew shape as black as night and as long as a man appeared out of thin air and impaled Rashatt through the stomach. The man gave a gurgled scream.

"GAAAAAAGH!"

Xelloss didn't blink. *"This* is why you can do nothing against me by yourself," he murmured as a second black corkscrew thrust through Rashatt's chest. Rashatt screamed and screamed, but Xelloss went on.

"Chaos Dragon created his own Priest and General to act as his minions, but Lord Greater Beast created me alone. I can make the math simple for you—Chaos Dragon split his power in two vessels while Lord Greater Beast left it all in one. Me."

"You and Priest Raltaak," Xelloss said in an almost disinterested tone, "had best combine your power against me, or else request that Sir Chaos Dragon come greet me in person." He ended his lecture by impaling another corkscrew through Rashatt's body.

I stared at Xelloss, then at the corkscrews, then at Xelloss again. My mind started piecing together the evidence of the unbelievable power I was witnessing.

Those corkscrews he wielded and the power to destroy an opponent without physically touching him. Did making them appear beyond the confines of space mean he was releasing that power from a point inside his opponent's body?

*Unless . . . wait.* Maybe the black corkscrews were Xelloss' *real body* on the Astral Plane.

A chill ran down my spine. Even though it was my current enemy writhing on Xelloss' corkscrews, it was only a matter of time before Xelloss turned on me. And when that time came . . .

I'd be screwed. Literally, if he used those awful things.

As the black corkscrews continued to impale Rashatt's body, Xelloss finally resumed talking.

"Forgive me for being hasty," he said, "but we can't dwell here long. A pity that we've only just met and now must part . . . forever." He chuckled, which proved to be deeply disturbing.

"What the hell is all this?!"

A familiar voice made me freeze. *No way,* I thought, my heart filling with dread. I turned slowly, my face preparing to wince.

Sure enough, Zelgadiss stood there with Gourry and Amelia by his side. The entire team's jaws had practically hit the floor.

Xelloss looked startled as he turned to us. When I glanced back at Rashatt, the general had disappeared—all that remained were the corkscrews floating in mid-air.

*Craptastic!*

"Hmm," Xelloss murmured, but he didn't seem very concerned. "He got away during a momentary opening. Ah, well—that's to be expected of the general, I suppose." He gave a little shrug, and the floating corkscrews dissolved into the wind.

I was pretty sure I could've fit an entire turkey in Zel's open mouth. "Wh-what the hell is all this?!" he stuttered at last. "What the hell is going on?! Xelloss!" He pointed at the priest. "Who the hell are *you?!*"

"He's not . . . a demon?!" Amelia squeaked in a tiny, high-pitched voice.

I sighed. The cat was out of the bag, apparently. Even people with a casual knowledge of sorcery would recognize an inhuman display of power like that.

I glanced over at Xelloss. He just raised an eyebrow at me expectantly.

*So this is my problem, huh? Thanks a lot, pal.*

I took a deep breath. "Okay," I said carefully, holding my hands out in peace. "I'll tell you everything I know, but

a little later, okay?" I gestured to the inferno around us. "We have to get out of here first."

My team agreed to that plan, at least. Fire has a way of getting people to move.

\*\*\*

The five of us—Xelloss included—left Galia as fast as we could. Since we wanted to get clear of the city without traveling too far, we settled in a hunting lodge at the foot of a nearby mountain.

That was when I told Gourry, Amelia, and Zelgadiss everything. All of the secrets I'd kept so awesomely poured out my mouth in one very long rant. I admitted that Xelloss was a demon, that he was taking me to the Claire Bible, and that the demon Rashatt had stuffed me in a palace room with promises of not killing me . . . and then had promptly tried to kill me. I added that Xelloss had been kind enough to save me from the small army of demons that had burned down Galia.

"This isn't funny," Zelgadiss said darkly.

"Thanks for clearing that up," I retorted dryly.

Amelia lowered her head. "So you knew about Mister Xelloss from the start?" she murmured.

"And you kept it from us." Zelgadiss glared at me.

*Duh,* I wanted to say. *Because I knew you'd all freak out if I told you. Way to prove that by freaking out!*

But they definitely had a point—I *had* been lying to them. That could be hard to take, even if the reasoning was practical (in my opinion).

Zelgadiss shifted his gaze from me to Xelloss. "So," Zel hissed. "What the hell are *you* planning?"

Xelloss had taken a chair in the corner of the lodge, by the way. He looked up from buffing his nails on his mantle and flashed Zel his usual smile.

"That's a secret," he hummed.

Zel jumped to his feet. "You dirty—"

"Stop it!" I snapped. Zelgadiss clenched his fists and aimed his blazing gaze back to me.

"Why should I?!" he shot back. "And why do you keep defending him?!"

*Because he could pick his teeth with my vertebrae, genius!*

I let out a long breath. "Zel," I said slowly, "Xelloss is extremely powerful. Probably more powerful than anyone else here."

I let that sink in for a minute. Zelgadiss, after glaring daggers at Xelloss, grumbled something and sat back down.

Amelia ventured a question. "What are you going to do now, Lina?"

*That* was what I liked to hear—planning for the future. Especially when my actions of the past were pissing off my teammates.

"Amelia's right," I declared. "Who cares who did what to whom? Onward to the future, I always say."

I quickly went on before anyone could interject. "First of all," I said, "I want to see this Claire Bible Xelloss keeps talking about. I know chasing after the carrot he's been dangling in front me is pretty lame . . ." I raised an eyebrow at Xelloss for emphasis. ". . . but finding out why demons are trying to murder me is more important than my pride. For now. So that's our next step."

Everyone went quiet for a minute. "I don't chase carrots," Zel muttered, although the analogy sounded pretty dumb when he rephrased it like that. "But I'd prefer it to running off and hiding with my tail between my legs."

Amelia nodded. "That goes for me, too. Now that we know Mister Xelloss is a demon, we can't just dance on the palm of someone given to darkness . . . but if it means protecting Lina, we need to look at unusual methods."

She folded her arms and nodded again, as if agreeing with herself. "Lina's certainly at the center of some plot, but we don't know if that plot is good or evil. We can't help it or hinder it until we discover that, right? Although it's a burden to play along with an evil scheme, it's a burden I'm willing to shoulder considering the circumstances."

Xelloss focused his attention over to Gourry. "And you, Mister Gourry?" he asked. "What do you intend to do?"

Gourry paused for a long moment, scratching his nose in thought. "Well," he said at last, "it's not like our situation's any different from yesterday."

Amelia practically popped. I wasn't surprised; Gourry was an idiot, and Amelia was an alarmist. We usually ended up having one of them freak during our meetings.

"Mister Gourry!" she cried as she ran up to get in his face. "Xelloss is a demon! *DEMON!* A creature wrapped in darkness, governed by fear and destruction, enemy to all living things! He is one hundred percent bad and zero percent good! You'd be traveling with a beast lower than the filthiest scum!"

Xelloss, in an odd moment, almost looked hurt.

Gourry wasn't fazed. "Sure," he said. "But I already figured he was a demon."

Every mouth in the room—save Gourry's—practically dropped to the floor. "WHAT?!" we screamed in perfect unison.

"You're *kidding* me!" I snapped, resisting the urge to grab him by the neck and start shaking. "*You* figured it out?! When? And how?!"

He smiled happily. "It's made more and more sense since we met him," he said like a commended schoolboy. "I can't really describe it, but it was like . . . his scent? Maybe? Anyway, I understood it somehow."

"Why didn't you say anything?" I demanded. "Or did you just keep traveling with him because you didn't mind?!"

Gourry shrugged. "Nah. I just figured that if you were keeping a stranger with you, you probably had a reason for it."

I stopped mid-insult and felt my eyes widen. I, Lina Inverse, was suddenly at a loss for words.

That meant . . . Gourry trusted me. *Really?* I thought. A thin tendril of happiness suddenly curled around my heart.

"I guess this means Mister Gourry plans to travel with Lina no matter what, then," Amelia commented from across the room.

Gourry smiled. "I'm her guardian, after all." He patted me on the head.

*Man, Gourry.*

Amelia glanced sharply at Xelloss. "I'm not sure what Mister Zelgadiss and I will do," she muttered, "but we can't make any hasty moves without knowing what *you* intend to do." She pointed at him dramatically. "So! Confess! We need to know your plans, Xelloss!"

Needless to say, Amelia's pressure didn't send Xelloss falling to knees in tears. He brushed a strand of hair behind his ear and lightly shook his head.

"I can't answer that," he said simply.

"Then you have a *reason* to not answer us! Maybe you're planning to use Lina to accomplish some evil deed!" I swear I saw Amelia's nostrils spew steam. "You can't play games with me, Xelloss! I have ways of making you talk!"

. . . This was sure to be good.

"Really," Xelloss murmured in mild interest. "And what ways might those be?"

Amelia beamed with a triumphant smile. "If you don't reveal all your plans this instant, I'll whisper happy words into your ears all night long—'life is beautiful' and 'love is blossoming' and 'kindness is its own reward'!"

Xelloss actually turned pale. "You wouldn't," he said softly.

Amelia threw back her head and laughed. "Of course!" she boomed. "Since you demons feed off the negative emotions of living things, praise for life must be hard for you to listen to!"

*It's not only demons who find that annoying,* I thought sourly.

Xelloss held up his hands palms-out, flustered. "B-but Hellmaster never told me the details!"

Amelia paused, a bit surprised, then squinted at Xelloss suspiciously. "He didn't tell you?" she clarified.

Xelloss nodded quickly. "It's the truth! Of the five retainers of Lord Ruby Eye Shabranigudu, four of them— Lord Hellmaster, Lord Deep Sea, Lord Dynast, and Chaos Dragon—all created Priests and Generals to serve them. But My Liege, Lord Greater Beast, created only me.

"By rights, Lord Hellmaster should be using his own priests to do the work he has assigned me lately. But, it's just . . ." He trailed off, then rubbed the back of his head and chuckled nervously. "His minions were all destroyed back in the Demon War a millennium ago. Rather inconvenient, don't you think?" He chuckled again.

79

It wasn't funny. What did Xelloss always think was so damn funny?

"Because of that, the task falls to me, the servant of Lord Greater Beast." Xelloss sighed. "But Lord Hellmaster has rather eccentric interests. He orders me to do this and that and go here and there, but he doesn't generally discuss the final objective of the operation."

Gourry slapped a fist into his palm. "Then you can't say, because you don't know!" he said triumphantly.

Clearly, Gourry hadn't considered that Xelloss might be lying.

Amelia, however, had practically snapped herself up in a Distrust Barrier. "Well?" she asked, turning to Zel and me. "What do you two think?"

"I don't buy it," Zel said flatly, rounding up our character clichés for the evening. "But I doubt we can get anything else out of him."

I shrugged. "And we've already learned a lot from what Xelloss has said so far," I added. When Amelia looked confused, I went on.

"I may not know why, but Chaos Dragon Gaav is working separately from the other demons. And he's the one after me."

"Excuse me?!" Xelloss spluttered. "And how did you jump to *that* conclusion?!"

I leveled my gaze at him. "Chaos Dragon is the only one you didn't call 'lord.'"

Xelloss stared at me, his lips parted. I'd knocked the guy dumb. My intellect can do that to people.

"You mentioned Chaos Dragon when you were fighting Rashatt, too," I added. "I still don't know where I fit in all this, but whatever Chaos Dragon's planning . . . I'm sure it's gonna be big."

Confusing little puzzle pieces had snapped together in my brain. Chaos Dragon, it looked like, considered humans a useful asset—maybe because he hated other demons, or maybe because he wanted to *overthrow* other demons.

But let me backtrack a little. Priest Raltaak, General Rashatt, and their boss, Chaos Dragon, may have been keeping their hands off innocent human bystanders for a while, but that didn't mean they considered humans allies. Explosive encounters that resulted in piles of dead innocents would attract the attention of Hellmaster and Xelloss, right? And they considered Hellmaster and Xelloss enemies. So staying away from big fights and thus under the radar meant their plans stayed secret from the demons they hated.

Of course, they probably wanted to leave open the option of a later demon-human alliance. I doubted that the old incident back in Saillune City and the events in Galia were because the demons were targeting me—I'd just barged my way into two plots to infiltrate the highest ranks of both nations. A classic example of wrong place, wrong time. Chaos Dragon and his subordinates probably wanted to control as many humans as possible through manipulating royal families. That way, if they ever engaged in a full-scale war with other demons, the humans might join in and serve as meat shields for Chaos Dragon.

This was all speculation, of course, but it made a lot of sense. And based on the look on Xelloss' face, I was at least on the right track.

Amelia gripped her chin. "Whatever the case," she said at last, "we have to play along for now, right? And that's how we'll get the truth." She threw a little glance at the quiet Xelloss, a tentative confidence twinkling in her eye. She'd probably liked watching me spook the guy.

"If I left now, it would nag at me later," Zelgadiss added. "So I'll stay to hear the whole story."

I nodded at the two of them. "Thanks, guys."

"Don't misunderstand us, Lina," Zelgadiss said evenly. "We'll go along with you for now, but when we find out what Xelloss and Chaos Dragon are up to . . ." He looked away. "I can't speak for Gourry, but Amelia and I may become your enemies."

I paused. It wasn't good news, but who was I to complain? My teammates were only with me because they chose to be.

"Fair enough," I murmured. I figured I'd cross *that* little bridge if we were unlucky enough to come to it.

I was getting a little antsy at that point, so I cracked my knuckles and turned to Xelloss. It was time to get moving—all that talk of coming to blows was getting a little uncomfortable.

"You," I said, pointing right between Xelloss' eyes. "No more games, okay? Where's the Claire Bible?"

Xelloss cleared his throat. "Nearby," he said in a very unexciting tone.

"And where exactly is 'nearby'?"

"At the Kataart Mountains that border this area. Dragon's Peak, to be precise." Xelloss looked out the window. "The Claire Bible lies within."

***

Dragon's Peak. If the rumors were true, the place was teeming with Gold and Black Dragons.

The five of us headed straight for the peak, avoiding the major highways as we did so. There was a giant, nameless forest on our way to the base of the mountain, and the only path through was a glorified game trail. Tree branches and the like had obviously been cut by bladed objects, lending truth to the rumors I'd heard of a "path to Dragon's Peak."

*How legendary,* I thought darkly as I tripped over another tree root. Considering the week I'd had, getting hit in the face with branches was the garnish on my crap steak.

Records in Galia's Sorcerers' Guild had said that, long ago, countless Gold and Black Dragons flooded the sky to converge at Dragon's Peak. Not counting the Deimos Dragons that dwell in the Kataart Mountains, Gold and Black Dragons are the two strongest kinds of dragons. Why they stayed huddled together on Dragon's Peak had never made sense to me.

It wasn't that they *couldn't* live anywhere else. I'd met Gold and Black Dragons in all kinds of weird places. Some sorcerers thought they stayed as a threat to the demons in Kataart . . . but considering the overwhelming power of demons—something the legends love to rub in—that didn't make much sense.

Until now, anyway. I had to admit, it was nice to be in on the secret.

*They're there for the Claire Bible.*

The dragons had probably assembled at Dragon's Peak to protect the thing. Which *also* meant we had our work cut out for us—the dragons wouldn't just hand the Bible over to a bunch of strangers and a powerful demon.

"Xelloss?" I asked as I squeezed through half-cut foliage. "If you know the dragons have the Claire Bible, why are you and the demons letting it sit there? Unless you have a reason to avoid Dragon's Peak . . ." I trailed off, hoping it would goad him into talking.

Xelloss, walking in the lead, didn't bother to turn around. "No," he replied. "I can't offer an exact reason for leaving the dragons be, but since the sorcery techniques in the Claire Bible are fundamentally similar to demonic powers, demons have little use for the thing. And we pick our battles, thank you."

"But you got rid of that manuscript when we fought the Ruby Eye cult," I reminded him. "And you said it'd be a threat to lower demons, if not you."

"That's if it fell into human hands." Xelloss snapped a branch that blocked his path. "Dragons are far more powerful than humans on average, and if they chose to utilize the Bible, they could indeed be a threat to demons. But out of instinct or confidence in their own powers, they don't use tools, acquire techniques, or record legends. They share that trait with demons, in fact.

"That distaste for tools will keep them from using the Claire Bible. But they also know better than to give it to humans indiscriminately." Xelloss waved a hand. "So their Bible is gathering dust."

"But—"

"Hey," Gourry suddenly said, cutting off my next question before I could ask it. He sniffed the air, then furrowed his eyebrows. "Does anyone else smell something burning?"

I was about to say, "Then you must be thinking too hard," but suddenly realized the situation could be serious. I stopped to take a deep sniff of the air. It was faint, maybe, but behind the piney scents of the forest was a faint charcoal smell.

Amelia was sniffing, too. "I think you're right!" she exclaimed.

That was when a huge chunk of the trees around us suddenly burst into flames.

FWOOM!

"Huh?!" I cried out in alarm as the others shouted around me. I instinctively jerked away from the branch I was pushing aside—it was burning now, as was its parent.

Xelloss seemed unbothered, but that was nothing new. As the rest of us huddled together and stared at the flames in shock, he looked beyond where we stood and murmured something.

"So this is your strategy?" he asked.

I whipped around to follow Xelloss' gaze. There, picking his way through the flame-engulfed trees, was my least favorite creepy old man.

"Raltaak?!" Amelia and I cried out at the same time.

*What is it with these guys and setting me on fire?!*

Raltaak had probably set the blaze from a distance to keep Xelloss from detecting him. With fire surrounding us, we were like penned pigs before the slaughter. Not a very *creative* technique, mind you, but definitely an effective one.

Raltaak shrugged. "Desperate times," he admitted, sounding a little embarrassed. Once he reached our ring of calm inside the fire, he leveled his gaze at Xelloss.

"I find coming to blows dreadfully tedious, wouldn't you say? I'd much rather attempt to first come to an arrangement." Those calm eyes turned to me. "If, for example, you were to let me dispose of the young lady . . ."

"No deal!" I shouted before anyone in the group could say something stupid. Since Xelloss had claimed to be out of information, I also figured this was a chance to try and pick Raltaak's brain. I had nothing to lose, anyway—I figured Xelloss would be pounding the guy within a minute.

"What exactly are you chasing me for?" I shouted over the roars of the fire. "I'm not about to roll over and die, but if we're after the same thing, I may considering *joining* you."

Xelloss looked at me in horror. "Miss Lina!" he reprimanded.

I ignored him. Was I the only one there with half a brain?

*I'm bluffing, you idiot.*

Raltaak paused a moment, his eyes falling on the hurt Xelloss. "One of my previous comrades was named Mazenda," he said after a moment.

"I figured," I said.

"I'm not certain where or how, but she one day came in possession of certain information: namely, that Hellmaster was moving forward on a rather large-scale project. Although she knew few details, one thing was clear." He looked at me again with a mixture of curiosity and some other, hard-to-define emotion. "A human by the name of Lina Inverse is a crucial part of this project."

*What?!*

"Let me get this straight," I said flatly. "You don't know what Hellmaster's up to, but to stop it you're gonna kill me? No questions asked?" I clenched my fists. "That's a cop-out, you cheap bastard!"

"It's a *precaution*," he tried to correct. "And your opinion on the matter doesn't make much difference."

I was ready to blast that cocky geezer through the fire and into orbit. I'm sure I don't have to say this, but here's a lesson for the day: NEVER MURDER SOMEBODY AS A PRECAUTION.

Those Mazoku assholes couldn't care less about human lives. I was an insect crawling across their nose—an insect they wanted to squish to avoid the possibility of getting bitten. I was starting to think they didn't even need that much justification.

SLAYERS: GAAV'S CHALLENGE

I was so pissed I could barely keep it in. My fists trembled at my sides as I ground my teeth together.

*You sick bastards.*

"I doubted the story from the beginning," Raltaak went on. "But then Kanzeil, who was working at the capitol of Saillune at the time, reported that a human of your description had arrived in his territory. We expected him to dispose of you just in case, so you can imagine our surprise when he was rather easily defeated.

"A mere human, defeating Kanzeil. And later, when Mazenda was destroyed along with the secret organization she had infiltrated, you held some connection to it." He shook his head. "I desired to meet you face to face. I fused Seigram—who already hated you—to a human who burned with the same malice. You remember that, I'm sure. I was surprised to learn that Sir Xelloss was by your side . . . and however it was manifesting, it seemed that Mazenda's information was correct."

"Sir Raltaak," Xelloss cut in quietly before Raltaak could say more. "This conversation has gotten long. Would you mind if we ended it here?"

Xelloss was right. The surrounding fire was fueled by the wind, so the flames pushed in at us. He may've been using a wind sink during his rant, considering he was a demon, and we weren't about to fall for it.

Raltaak touched his chin. "Perhaps I have talked too long," he admitted. "But the fact remains that I can't let the young lady escape."

The second he said the words, another figure emerged from the flames behind him. I knew it was General Rashatt before the guy was all the way through, but what I didn't expect was what he looked like now.

Instead of the silvery armor of Dilse Kingdom, he was decked out in reddish-black armor with dragon features. The naked sword in his hand was a larger version of his demonic blade from earlier. I guessed that his get-up was his usual Mazoku wear.

"So we meet again, General." Xelloss pursed his lips. "You don't look well—has your health not recovered yet?"

Rashatt's eyes lit up with anger, but he kept his mouth shut.

Needless to say, considering the increasing heat and the encroaching fire, I wanted nothing more than to get the hell out of there. Now I had to think my past *two* angry Mazoku.

Xelloss shrugged. "I think that with Mister Rashatt in such condition," he told Raltaak, "you two can't defeat me, even if you do join forces."

"I'm aware," Raltaak said in his usual simplicity. "But we can also keep you occupied while this blaze engulfs the girl."

*What?! Hey!*

"We can't have that," Xelloss said without turning his eyes from his enemy. "Everyone, please—be sure to take care of Miss Lina."

As the three Mazoku were locked in a death glare, miasma and bloodlust filled the already sweltering air. The instant I thought something was sure to snap, the three of them vanished.

*The Astral Plane. Right.* They probably wanted to fight with their real bodies.

I didn't waste any time. "Okay!" I called, turning to the others and planting my fists on my hips. "We're getting out of here while they're in their own world."

"But how?!" Amelia was starting to panic. "We can't put out a fire this big. Using Levitation will just get us roasted on top of the flames, and you're the only one who can use Ray Wing!"

"Easy," I replied. "We'll make a wind barrier everyone can get inside. We'll cast a minor cold spell in it to keep us protected."

Zelgadiss looked out at the flames. "Like in Sairaag," he commented.

He was right. I'd done this before—we'd be fine if we concentrated our defensive powers to boost the barrier.

Gourry spread his feet. "Got it," he declared. "So then I'll just . . . um . . ."

"You'll shut up and get in, Gourry." I mimicked Zel and scanned the fire around us. "Somehow I doubt Raltaak counted on a fire to do us in, so there may be another enemy nearby. I'd like to be free to use my offensive magic."

"Then we'll leave that to you!" Amelia offered, a new, confident smile tugging at her lips. "You're the one with the biggest repertoire of black magic here. I'll do the barrier and cold spell . . . and could you reinforce the barrier and take care of our movement, Mister Zelgadiss?"

Zel nodded his affirmative as Amelia began chanting. After a decently big wind barrier enveloped the four of us, Zel proceeded to reinforce it; whether there was a threat outside the fire or not, it wouldn't pay to be stupid. Zel eventually took control of the barrier sphere and lifted us into the air.

I let out a breath as soon as we were clear of the flames. *That was getting too hot for my tastes,* I thought as I watched the scene below us. We flew over the fire in the direction of Dragon's Peak, leaving a forest fire in our magical wake.

I'm sure we looked incredible. Well . . . we either looked incredible or incredibly irresponsible about proper forest safety.

The flames did reach up to touch our barrier from time to time, but the cold spell inside the barrier kept it comfortably cool. I daresay we were almost traveling in style.

"Incoming!" Gourry yelled.

My temporary relaxation went out the window as three shadows shot up from the burning forest. They halted in mid-air, roughly encircling our wind barrier.

They were Mazoku, obviously—one wore a black mask and a white robe, another had a blue face, and the third had a body like a wispy, blue cloud. Their bodies looked like water or ice molded into human form.

We outnumbered them, and they weren't as powerful as Raltaak or Rashatt, but they were still pretty threatening when we were missing Xelloss. *And* I was the only one who could cast spells, since Amelia and Zel were in charge of the barrier. I wished we were on the ground—we would've had a good chance of winning.

*Can I use Gourry?* I wondered. Gourry had the Sword of Light, which formed a blade of light from the bearer's will and was more than effective against demons. But legendary or not, it was still a sword; it would do zilch for attacks that came from outside the barrier.

I had to hand it to Raltaak. Between the fire, the reinforcements, and the fact that the reinforcements could break our barrier and send us plummeting *back* into the fire, we were pretty screwed.

I was left with one option: blasting through those demons as fast and as hard as possible. I chanted my spell, glaring at the white one.

"Ragna Blast!" I shouted . . . and blasted the one with the blue face in the back. It was a pretty awesome feint, if I do say so myself, and it worked perfectly.

Five black pillars enveloped the Mazoku in mid-air, extending tentacles of black plasma over his entire body. With a single, quick shudder, the demon melted into the darkness.

*That's one.*

The white guy and the wispy guy attacked in unison after that. They spawned a number of lances of light and fired them straight at me; since the lances slid through the barrier, I jerked back to get out of the way.

That's when I remembered there's not much footing in a bubble. I hate to admit it, but I squawked in surprised and bowled over spectacularly.

*Dammit!* At least the lances passed over my head, since I'd essentially ducked. I began casting the next spell as I struggled to my feet.

A blue form suddenly appeared in front of me in the barrier. I gave a start when I realized it was the demon I'd already killed, a ball of magic light burning in his right palm.

"H-hey!" I shouted in a panic. Not only was he not dead, he was in my personal space!

SLICE!

Light bisected the demon from head to toe. The guy roared as his two halves split and then vanished into thin air. I whipped around to face Gourry in surprise. I hadn't seen him draw his sword, but there it was, blazing in his hands. He gestured to the demons outside with his head.

"Now he's dead for good," he said. "Two more, Lina!"

I nodded and continued my chanting. This time I turned to the white Mazoku in front.

"Dragon Slave!" I shouted.

A blazing red ray roared toward the demon, making our wind barrier shudder. The demon vanished just before the red light could converge on a point.

*Not again!* I thought angrily. Those infuriating Mazoku were probably slipping in and out of the Astral Plane.

The wispy Mazoku had taken that time to drop below the wind barrier. Before he could shoot lances up at us from under our feet, Gourry pointed his Sword of Light to the base of the barrier.

"Beat it!" he shouted as he fired the light blade straight through the barrier and at the demon. I wish I'd known he could do that earlier.

The Mazoku evaded the light, but the movement forced him out of his position below us. It was good enough for the moment. I used the time to chant my next spell—that slippery white bastard was sure to come back. He had perfect timing, since I completed my spell just as he popped back into the Material Plane.

Unfortunately, it was inside the barrier and right behind Amelia.

Gourry must've sensed his presence, because he jerked around with his sword raised. But neither Gourry nor I could use the power we'd built up because anything we shot would hit the demon *and* Amelia.

My palms began to sweat. Amelia turned to the demon just as he formed a lance of light.

"Amelia!" Gourry shouted.

CRRCKSH.

With a really odd sound, the white demon's head crumbled into little pieces. The lances he'd been forming vanished as he died.

*Huh?*

I was dumbstruck. Gourry hadn't killed that guy, and I *definitely* hadn't killed that guy. With Amelia and Zel doing the barrier spells, who had killed the demon? I glanced over at the wispy Mazoku hovering outside, but he looked just as shocked as the rest of us.

Oh, well—back to work.

"DRAGON SLAVE!" I cried.

The last demon was vaporized in a vast, scarlet explosion that left deafening sound to reverberate through our barrier. Say what you will about violence, but there's nothing quite as beautiful as a Dragon Slave blasting someone who's trying to kill you.

I let out a breath in relief. "Okay," I said as I turned to my party. "Disaster avoided for the moment. Everyone in one piece?"

Gourry frowned. "What happened to the white one, Lina?"

I paused. "Xelloss, if I had to guess," I admitted. "He probably used an opening in the Astral Plane battle with Raltaak and Rashatt to intervene here."

Xelloss was good in a pinch, but he'd been an absolute lifesaver as of late. I was really, really thankful he was on our side and on overtime.

With Raltaak's demon thugs properly blown into oblivion, the four of us continued our flight over the flames to Dragon's Peak.

***

"He's not here yet," Amelia mumbled, clearly bored out of her mind.

I grumbled an affirmative and looked up at the clear blue sky.

It was a warm, sunny morning, behind us stood a charcoal-burner's cabin and the looming Dragon's Peak.

It had been three days since the fight. Heavy rain while we were traveling had forced us to make camp in the forest that first night, but the rain had put out the fires enough that we could find non-burning tree cover. We'd arrived at the base of Dragon's Peak the next morning and had since sat there on our butts.

"He's not here yet," Amelia intoned again in her apathetic gurgle.

We hadn't seen hide nor hair of Xelloss. Since he was the reason we had to stay put, a popular pastime was complaining about him.

It's true that there are things to do at the base of a mountain peak—fish, walk, hunt, whatever—but since we knew a demonic army sent by Raltaak could pop up anywhere, we had to stay together and in one place.

Unfortunately, we had no idea when Xelloss would appear, and gazing into the forest in the hopes of seeing him was a waste. Popping in and out of the Astral Plane implied that he wouldn't be *walking* over to where we were.

But we stared into the forest anyway. What else were we gonna do?

"Still not here, huh?" I heard Gourry walk over from the cabin behind us. He stopped at my back. "Lina?"

"No," I murmured distractedly.

Gourry stood there a second, then sat down beside me and looked out at the fire. He was zoning out in a fraction of the time it had taken me to go brain dead.

Well . . . that made sense. Next to swordplay, zoning out was Gourry's specialty.

After a few minutes, he asked, "Do you think those guys got him?"

I licked my teeth. "It's possible. But whatever happened, we're getting nowhere fast without him."

"How about we go to Dragon's Peak on our own?"

I turned to him and raised an eyebrow. "And do what once we get there?"

Gourry scratched his head. "Weren't you looking for something there?" he asked. "I thought that was why we're going."

I sighed and turned back to the forest fire. "Not gonna happen, Gourry. The Claire Bible's protected by dragons, and I doubt they're willing to share."

"What if you explained the circumstances?"

Oh, *that* was a good idea.

"Sure," I said sarcastically. "I'll waltz in there, introduce myself, and tell them Xelloss the demon sent me. Oh, and I'll add that he's planning something with me and the Bible—I'm sure they'll hand the thing right over."

Gourry dropped his head. "Honesty's the best policy," he said in a dejected tone.

"You should know that saying's a lie by now, Gourry."

To be honest, I was ready to throw in the towel at Dragon's Peak. If Xelloss didn't show, I planned to up and walk away from the whole dragon-and-Bible mess . . . but I doubted I could use the same tactic with Chaos Dragon and his henchmen. Leaving the mountain wouldn't help me get rid of them.

I needed Xelloss back. Or a good plan. Or a *clue*, even.

Amelia leaned back on her arms. "Let's wait one more day," she suggested. "If he doesn't come tomorrow, we'll reevaluate."

The second she finished talking, a shadow passed over us in time with a gust of wind. A loud beating sound filled the air.

FLAP, FLAP.

TOWARD THE LEGENDARY PEAK OF DRAGONS

I looked up in surprise. There, landing just steps away, was a shining Gold Dragon.

Although the smallest of all dragons, Gold Dragons' abilities were still the most impressive, giving them the title of "Dragon Lords." Their hides were impervious to dull swords, and their minds could comprehend multiple languages while still commanding the strongest of spells.

A single Laser Breath from their maws could split a Red Dragon's body in two.

Zelgadiss probably heard the disturbance, because he left the cabin and ran over. The dragon, meanwhile, slowly bent his neck to look down at the four of us.

After everything I'd been through, it took more than a Gold Dragon to impress me. "What do you want?" I asked him bluntly.

The dragon shifted his gaze to focus on me alone. "I mean to ask you the same question," he replied in human language. Some of his words were hard to pick up, probably because of his different body size and vocal chords.

"No way!" Gourry jumped to his feet, his eyes wide in shock. He turned to me like an excited toddler and pointed repeatedly at our new guest.

"Did you hear that?!" he cried. "The dragon can talk, Lina!"

*Way to be uncultured, Gourry.*

"Of course he can," I said dryly. "What did you expect him to do? Make smoke signals?"

Okay, that was a little funny.

"Ah," the dragon said, turning his attention to Gourry. "Is it rare for dragons to speak?" The dragon almost seemed amused by Gourry's fascination.

Gourry rubbed the back of his head in embarrassment. "Um . . . well, it's the first time *I've* see a dragon talk. Mister Gold Dragon, sir." He gripped his chin. "How'd you learn to talk like humans, anyway?"

The dragon gave a long, low hum. "We dragons live longs lives. Toying with the words of other organisms is a way to pass the time."

"Then you learned 'cause you were bored?"

"I suppose you could say that." The dragon redirected his attention to the entire group again. "As I was saying, humans. What are you doing in a place like this, especially when you're sedentary for days at a time?"

*Not by choice,* I retorted internally. Like we wanted to sit on our asses all day!

"Although some humans come at times to make your 'charcoal' material, you don't appear to be doing that. This is a peak where dragons reside; if you have no business, you must leave."

I exchanged glances with Amelia and Zel. Gourry was too busy geeking out over the dragon, so I left him to his own devices.

"We're . . . waiting for someone," I told the dragon at last. And before anyone in the group—particularly Gourry—could throw the no-no word *demon* in there, I quickly added, "We were split up from someone we were traveling with and figured we'd wait here until he showed up."

"In this place?" the dragon asked.

I wasn't covering very well. Why couldn't dragons be really *dumb* creatures of myth?

"It's not that we promised to meet up here," I offered. "But we were in the area, you know? So we just picked a place to wait."

"Really?" the dragon asked again, clearly not taking my word for it.

"Really," Xelloss answered.

*Huh?!* I jumped to my feet. A familiar black-robed figure stepped out from behind the dragon.

"Xelloss!" I called.

Xelloss tipped his head politely. "Sorry to keep you waiting so long."

I was glad he was alive—and possibly even happier he was back in our party. "What happened to you-know-who and his other half?" I asked.

Xelloss shrugged. "We couldn't settle things this time, either, so we just battled until they managed to escape. I considered pursuing, but, well . . ." He chuckled. "It seemed like too much trouble."

Wait. Then that meant he'd been fighting until *right then?!*

"Anyway," Xelloss said before I had time to comment. He turned to the Gold Dragon. "I have a favor I'd like to ask of you. Do you mind if we enter your den?"

The dragon didn't give Xelloss any slack, either. "Our den?" he repeated. "For what purpose?"

"It's related to—oh, and while I'm thinking of it, may I speak to your elder directly? How is Mister Milgazia these days?"

It was the dragon's turn to feel a little of the Xelloss Freak-Out Factor. "The elder?" he asked unbelievably. "How do *you* know the elder?"

Xelloss smiled. "He's . . . an old acquaintance, we'll say. Tell him Xelloss has a request; I'm sure he'll understand."

The dragon looked at Xelloss suspiciously. "Who are you?" he asked slowly, his tone implying that Xelloss wasn't human.

Xelloss raised his right index finger. "That's a secret," he chimed.

*Wow,* I thought. *Xelloss just used his Secret Attack!*

The dragon paused. "Very well," he said at last. "I'll speak to the elder, so wait until I return." With a swooping of his neck and a flapping of his massive wings, the dragon took off into the sky and eventually vanished over the high peak.

Gourry turned to Xelloss once the dragon was gone. "Do you really know the dragon boss?" he asked.

Xelloss smiled at the question. "In a way, yes. I met him briefly quite some time ago."

"Whoa." Gourry whistled. "You're pretty famous, Xelloss."

"I'm older than I look, you know."

"How old *are* you?"

Xelloss laughed at that. "Now, now, Mister Gourry," he said with a click of his tongue. "It's rude to ask a lady her age."

*Um . . . YIKES.*

I tuned the two of them out as their conversation grew more ridiculous. Xelloss was just batting off another question when the air suddenly quivered.

The sky darkened over us, but in a far wider area than before. I looked up, blinked, then rubbed my eyes to make sure I was seeing right.

The sky was *filled* with dragons. Hundreds or even thousands of Gold and Black Dragons blanketed the sky in some sort of twisting, dizzying dance. A single beast among them slowly descended to where we stood.

He was another Gold Dragon, but he was substantially bigger than the one from earlier. He was probably a lot older and more powerful, too—the guy could've been several millennia old, even. He made sure to touch ground directly in front of Xelloss.

The dragon gazed at Xelloss with obvious suspicion and distaste. That meant they really *had* met.

"It's been a while, Mister Milgazia," Xelloss said cheerfully.

"Yes," the dragon replied in disgust. "Although I was hoping we'd never meet again after the Demon War, Priest Xelloss."

# 3: THE GOLDEN KING OF DARKNESS

**W**hat do you want?" the Gold Dragon, Milgazia, asked Xelloss flatly. The words ended up sounding more like a threat than a question.

I didn't blame the guy.

If the legends were true, dragons and Mazoku were serious enemies—they were on opposite sides during the Demon War. And since Milgazia had mentioned that war specifically, there was a good chance those legends had a *lot* of truth to them.

*Especially considering the look on his face*, I added silently. Milgazia glared at Xelloss like a barmaid who'd found a rat.

Still, Milgazia hadn't attacked or anything. Maybe he was putting aside the past for business.

"I have a little business with the Claire Bible," Xelloss said, basically repeating my thoughts out loud. "You don't mind, do you?"

"What would a demon want with it?" Milgazia snapped.

"It's not for me," Xelloss explained, gesturing to me as he did so. "I'd just like this human woman to use it a bit."

"A human . . . ?" The elder Gold Dragon stared at me skeptically. He turned back to Xelloss. "What is your scheme here, Priest?"

Xelloss held a hand palm-up in a defeated gesture. "It's Lord Hellmaster who's scheming, and I don't know his objective. My office dictates that I have no choice but to obey."

"And if I refuse?" Milgazia asked.

"I'll think of some means other than diplomacy," Xelloss answered calmly. He didn't flinch under Milgazia's glare.

After a long staring contest, Milgazia finally sighed. "So be it," he said dryly. "We don't have the means to stop you, so we have to let you do as you please."

"That's very kind of you," Xelloss said politely, which was one of his best bits of bull yet.

"However." Milgazia's voice was a sharp warning. "I will accompany you to watch."

*This oughta be fun,* I thought sarcastically.

The elder dragon lifted his head and let loose with a piercing cry. His body shuddered, then burst into a gold-colored cloud that trembled as it shrank. A few seconds later, Milgazia had morphed into an entirely new form.

For all intents and purposes, he looked like a human. He was blond, middle-aged, and reasonably attractive, blue clothing wrapped around him.

I was impressed. *That cry was a metamorphosis spell,* I thought.

"Follow me," Milgazia said before turning his back to us.

I reminded myself to be on my best behavior.

\*\*\*

Our party of six—four humans and two miscellaneous—headed along a mountain path cut from raw stone. We were silent, and had been since leaving the base of the peak; no matter what questions we had, we knew better than to ask.

I made sure to take in the decidedly unique surroundings as we walked. I could see dragons watching us from distant cliffs and outcroppings and wondered if they were afraid of something.

Milgazia stayed in the lead, adamant about not turning around to grace us with his gaze. His back practically shouted, "P'tooie to any human following that asshole demon!" (I paraphrased that, of course.)

The silence started to get to me after a while. I had a mountain of burning questions and a bunch of legendary creatures to direct them at, but we were all staying clammed up because Milgazia was being pissy.

*Where's the Claire Bible?!* was the main thing I wanted to screech at the top of my lungs. But could I ask without getting in trouble? At best, Milgazia would ignore me. At worst . . . well, I didn't want to think that far. But since I was on the top of the guy's suck list, I needed someone else to break the ice.

That moment, Gourry, of all people, opened his mouth. "Xelloss?" he asked as he turned to our fifth party member.

Milgazia twitched at Gourry's voice. I doubted an elder dragon enjoyed discussions behind his back that involved enemies he couldn't kill.

"Yes?" Xelloss replied, his tone buoyant to Gourry's casual.

"You must be, like, one of the oldest farts ever."

Amelia, Zelgadiss, and I froze in our tracks. Even Xelloss halted to stare at Gourry.

"Excuse me?"

Gourry scratched his head. "Um, Mister Dragon mentioned the Demon War, and I think I've heard of that before. It was a long time ago, right?"

Xelloss swallowed his surprise. "To be more precise," he said with a slightly forced smile, "it was around twelve hundred years ago."

"So that means you're at least that old. Huh." Gourry stroked his chin. "I guess I can see why you don't like talking about it. Don't worry, though—you don't look a day over twenty."

Gourry's thought processes never ceased to amaze. I dropped my head in my hands.

*Thank you for wasting our precious chance to ask a question, Gourry!*

By the way—from a demon's perspective, Xelloss wasn't old at all. And I doubted that Xelloss' appearance was his true form, anyway.

"Er . . . thank you," Xelloss said, clearly unsure of what to say.

Since I couldn't count on Gourry to pick Milgazia's brain, I had to find an opening myself. I noticed that the dragon had stopped to turn and stare at Gourry like the rest of us.

*Here's my chance!* I cleared my throat and smiled at the dragon.

"Don't worry, Mister Milgazia," I assured him. "He's always like this." Making fun of Gourry was always a good icebreaker.

"I . . . see," was his ambiguous reply. He turned around and kept walking.

He couldn't get rid of me that easily. "Mister Milgazia," I ventured casually. "I've been meaning to ask you: how do so many dragons live here? Is there a special food supply or something?"

Dragon's Peak had about the same amount of topsoil and large trees as the side of a volcano. There were small animals that fed on tree seeds and all, but that didn't seem nearly good enough to feed a flock of dragons.

Milgazia paused. "We neither require nor desire much food," he said coldly. "Dragons need normal amounts of food while young, but naturally learn how to derive nourishment from wind and sunlight over time.

"Although," he added, "we do still need to eat, and that must occur at least monthly. Just bear in mind that if we ate more, the world's resources would have run out long ago."

That made sense. "All right," I said. "Interesting."

"Now *I* have a question, human girl." I could hear the ice prickling from his words. "If you know Xelloss is a demon and up to some scheme, why are you cooperating with him?"

I took a breath. "It's a survival thing," I explained. "I don't know what Xelloss and Hellmaster Phibrizzo are planning, but I know that it has something to do with me. Since there's another Mazoku faction out there that's just as clueless as I am but still wants to kill me to stop Xelloss, I don't have much choice but to stay with him for now.

"I know that Hellmaster isn't a 'world peace' kind of guy," I said as a disclaimer. "And the demons trying to kill me may be more in the right, in this case. But I'm not the kind of girl to sit back and die for no good reason."

Milgazia was silent for a moment. "Don't be ashamed of your natural instinct to survive," he said at last. His tone was even and he didn't look at me, but for some reason I felt like he kinda understood.

"This is only temporary." I shook out my mantle. "I don't like being manipulated, so I'll only do it to find out the truth. And since those demons who want my hide aren't giving up anytime soon, and since my death may *not* stop Hellmaster's plan, giving up and getting killed now may end up being a spectacularly useless death."

Milgazia slowly turned his head to me for the first time since our meeting. "Should you be talking about this in front of him?" he asked, glancing at Xelloss.

Xelloss just smiled again. "I don't mind," he hummed. "And I expected nothing less from her than a thorough consideration of the circumstances."

"Mm." The elder Gold Dragon fell into thought for a while. When he finally spoke again, it was about me. "What concerns me is this: human girl—Lina, was it?— perhaps you are one of the seven dispersed parts of Ruby Eye Shabranigudu."

I froze. "What?!" I exclaimed, in perfect unison with my teammates. We'd been doing that a lot lately.

Everyone knew the old story. The Demon King Ruby Eye Shabranigudu was split into seven pieces and sealed after his duel with our world's god, Ceipheed the Red Dragon God. Ceipheed—who was badly injured in the fight—vanished from the world after leaving four offshoots of himself while the Demon King scattered Mazoku across the world. Later, during the Demon War, one of the sealed pieces of Ruby Eye descended onto the Kataart Mountains and destroyed one of Ceipheed's extensions: the Water Dragon King.

The Demon War was over a thousand years ago. Fast-forward to a little over a year ago, when I saw the second Ruby Eye seal unlocked with my own eyes. That meant there were five sealed pieces still scattered around somewhere.

Milgazia thought I was one of *those*?!

I was shocked stupid for a second. "Wh-what?" I finally managed. "What do you mean by that?!"

Milgazia's tone didn't change. "I was under the impression that humans are aware of how Ruby Eye's seven pieces were sealed."

"Well . . . that part of the story's pretty famous, yeah."

"Ceipheed sealed Shabranigudu within the 'souls' that humans possess. When one of those humans dies, the Demon King fragment is reborn in another.

"A seal within a dragon or an elf would have been stronger, of course. But he deliberately chose humans, likely because the infinite reincarnations of the humans' much shorter life cycle might little by little purify and annihilate the Demon King through the human soul."

Milgazia let out a slightly heavier breath. "But the power of humans is weak indeed. If the seal is weak, Hellmaster, through his ability to 'see' reincarnations, may become aware of it.

"He would likely move to release that seal; Hellmaster was the one who released the seal at the time of the Demon War, after all. And now he has a new plot.

"You understand my reasoning now," he said matter-of-factly.

I swallowed hard.

"Then . . . the Claire Bible is the key to removing the seal?" I asked faintly.

Milgazia shook his head. "No; the Claire Bible is simply knowledge that flows from another world. Even if you are indeed a piece of the Demon King, it will not remove the seal in and of itself.

"It could be part of some process, however. Or Hellmaster's plan could be something else entirely."

That little bit at the end didn't do much for my racing heart. Shouldn't drop a bomb like "Maybe you're a seventh of Darkness!" and expect the classic "or not" excuse to bring down the tension in the room.

"E-either way," I murmured. "We won't know what the Bible's for until we know what Hellmaster's after."

"Precisely. But fear not—if you believe in yourself, the path you must follow will become traversable . . . Here." Milgazia suddenly halted at a completely featureless ascending slope. It was about as wide as a road, had a steep cliff to the right and some shrubs to the left, and led to a downward slope that was pretty much a sheer drop.

It didn't make sense. "Here?" I asked carefully.

"Here." The Gold Dragon suddenly slipped half his body into the cliff to our right.

*Ah.*

"The Claire Bible lies within," he said. "This may appear to be a cliff, but you can walk through it normally. Come with me, Lina." He glanced at the others. "I ask that the rest of you stay here."

"Why just Lina?" Amelia asked.

Milgazia brought his whole body out of the wall once more. "My agreement with the priest is to take this girl to the Claire Bible. I don't wish to take any more humans. You can follow if you please, but you'll be alone if you lose your way."

"Lose our way?" Gourry frowned. "Then it's like a maze inside there?"

"One could call it that," Milgazia replied. "There are nearly an infinite number of branches, and even I only remember the way in and out. A demon or dragon could find his way back, but a human would be lost until his final breath."

It was a pretty good deterrent. Gourry, Zel, and Amelia looked at each other.

"We'll wait for you here, Lina," Zelgadiss said quietly.

Gourry nodded. "Be careful and come back soon, okay?"

"Get me a souvenir?" Amelia asked.

I was a little miffed that my party was ready to ditch me so soon, but following along was way too dangerous. I sighed and gave them a shrug.

Milgazia's gaze darkened at Xelloss. "You remain here," he said. "See that they do not change their minds."

Xelloss grinned. "Understood."

That one threw me a little. I stared at Xelloss incredulously.

"You're kidding me," I snapped. "After everything you did to drag me here, now you're fine having no idea what I do when I get to the Bible?"

Xelloss twirled a finger in the air. "If you must ask," he said, "my sole duty was to safely bring you to the location of the Claire Bible. This is essentially the same thing, and I have no idea what to do beyond this point, anyway."

*He's honest—I'll give him that.* But if *my* boss was Hellmaster Phibrizzo, I'd probably take my jobs more seriously.

Whatever. If he was going to be brush-off, he could do it on his own time.

"Come, Lina." Milgazia held out a palm.

I nodded. After drawing in a deep breath, I took the dragon's hand.

\*\*\*

The second we passed through the cliff, I got a *very* bad feeling. It was like . . . my body didn't belong to me or something.

Actually, "bad feeling" really doesn't do it justice. It's impossible to describe how I felt just then—it was nothing like anything else I'd ever experienced, and I'd been in some weird situations before this.

"Wh-what's with this place?" I murmured as Milgazia led me forward. I looked around; the surroundings made about as much sense as my feelings at the time.

The cave should've been lined with bare rock, but it seemed to be made of anything but. Stranger still, every time I got distracted or looked away for a moment, everything changed—the passage looked like it was made of crystal, then of flat stone, then of the belly lining of some giant, living creature.

*Is this place crazy?* I wondered. *Or did I hit my head on the way in?*

"Do not be concerned," Milgazia said as he led me through an upside-down passage.

I swallowed. "Now I *am* worried," I said. "I wish you hadn't told me not to worry."

Milgazia was suddenly right-side-up again. But now he didn't look like a dragon man—he looked like a giant pea, for some reason, unbothered and off in the distance. This was all while I could still feel him holding my left hand, so the experience was really bizarre.

I was worried. A lot. And now it had nothing to do with what Milgazia said or didn't say.

"Trust the sensation of my hand, Lina." His voice came from somewhere. "If you rely on your eyes, they will deceive you."

*His hand?*

I looked at my left hand. As I shifted my gaze to the hand he gripped it with—

There he was again, a dragon man, walking normally beside me.

I was going to remember that trick.

"This place," he explained, "dates back along time ago to the appearance of the Claire Bible during the Demon War. The power of the shockwave from when Ruby Eye and the Water Dragon King were destroyed is probably what altered the spatial integrity. The nature of this place is closest to that of the Astral Plane."

"Really?"

He nodded. "What you see and hear is not via your eyes and ears, but with your mind. Anxiety will turn a flower garden into hell or a soft wind into the screams of the dead. Hostility, bloodlust, and despair turn into destruction."

*Huh. So you're only as strong as your will.* But if that was the case . . . why had I seen Milgazia as a giant pea? What part of my psyche was *that?*

"It's all a facet of the nature of this place. Even a demon of middle rank would find it difficult to escape if he became lost here." He paused. "My own circumstances would be similar."

I cleared my throat. "Then, um, please don't get us lost."

"I already have," he said gravely.

I screamed—a high-pitched, girly little scream. Hey, I earned it.

Milgazia waited until I was finished. "That was a joke, Lina."

I stared at him with wide eyes. A joke? A joke?! There are some jokes in this world that are *never, ever funny!*

*Ugh,* I thought. *As if I didn't have enough to freak out about without an old guy who makes the funnies.*

"I apologize for the funnies," Milgazia responded.

It took me a second to realize I hadn't said my last line out loud. We could hear each other's thoughts in that place?

I needed to be careful. I couldn't think my usual running commentary about how stupid and ugly dragons were.

"Would you like me to leave you behind?"

"Now *I'm* kidding," I said. "Are we at the Claire Bible yet?"

"A little farther. And I wanted to ask you, incidentally . . . why do you desire its otherworldly knowledge at all?"

I shrugged. "I said it earlier, didn't I? I'm not playing along with Xelloss and Hellmaster forever. But since that means I'll have to fight them someday, I want to get my hands on a power that I can pull out last-minute on them."

"That's not possible," he practically sighed in response, his voice unusually tired.

I raised an eyebrow. "I do a lot of things that aren't possible."

"No matter how much otherworldly knowledge you obtain, Lina, there is only so much a human can control. In a direct battle, you would likely lose to Xelloss, and you would certainly lose to Hellmaster."

I scratched behind my ear. "I understand that Xelloss is pretty tough, but I—"

"You understand *nothing.*" This time Milgazia made a very real and very long sigh. "Why do you think I agreed to Xelloss' request to bring you here so easily?"

I was a little surprised by the question. "Uh . . . I know it wasn't because you guys are friends, but—"

"I'm *afraid* of him, Lina."

*Huh?* I opened my mouth, but then shut it again. Had I just heard him right?

Milgazia was an elder Gold Dragon, a *Dragon Lord*. I knew that Xelloss was insanely powerful, but no way would a Dragon Lord piss his pants at the sight of him.

"During the Demon War," Milgazia murmured, "over a millennium ago . . . he almost sent the race of dragons into extinction. By himself."

I felt like someone had hit me in the back of the head. "You're joking," I choked out.

"No. If I had refused his request, he would have surely killed all the Gold and Black Dragons of this peak and then found a way to bring you to the Bible himself. It would have inconvenienced him, certainly, but it would have been within the realm of his capability. I chose not to resist to protect the lives of my comrades."

He wasn't joking. Based on how tight I could see him clenching his jaw, Milgazia was honestly scared of Xelloss.

I'd always thought that the old legend of a single demon crushing all the dragons was the result of snowballing rumors. Not only was it true, apparently, but that legend was talking about *Xelloss*.

That was WAY more power than I'd ever expected him to have. I was starting to think Xelloss' abilities were beyond my wildest dreams.

"We couldn't defeat him in battle," Milgazia went on. "Not even with all of us united as a single force. But escaping is a possibility, depending on the circumstances."

I swallowed hard. My life was suddenly looking a whole lot shorter.

"Thanks for the advice," I murmured. "I'll, uh, do my best."

We walked in silence after that. I mean, what was I gonna say? The situation was awkward, and I was feeling a little queasy, so I decided to keep both my mouth shut and my mind unfocused. He could hear me if I started thinking too much, after all.

After a little while, Milgazia stopped in an arbitrary spot. "We've arrived at last," he declared.

I hadn't noticed anything in the area, but I glanced around again to make sure. All I found was more nonsensical space.

"Here?" I asked him. "I don't see anything."

"Here." He pointed to a spot in mid-air.

An *empty* spot. So first the whole "expanse of the mind" thing made the giant peas (?) in my subconscious take over, and now we'd found a non-existent Bible?

*I can't take many more of these head trips.*

The Gold Dragon seemed to notice my confusion. "Hmm," he said after a moment. "Perhaps human eyes cannot see it. If that is the case, try to 'sense' what is there."

I frowned. Sense it? How was I supposed to do that? Since I couldn't see the thing anyway, I closed my eyes to narrow my focus.

And there it was. I *saw* it the second I closed my eyelids.

My eyes popped back open. The space in front of me was still empty, but now I . . . it may sound weird, but I knew it was there without seeing it. And I knew it was an orb, big enough to fit perfectly between the palms of my hands.

"The orb?" I asked, reaching into the air and gingerly touching it.

"Not an orb." An unfamiliar voice hung in the air. "But the origin point at the center of this warped, chaotic

space through which otherworldly knowledge flows. You call this the Claire Bible."

I quickly jerked my hand back. *Who said that?* I wondered. I hadn't recognized the voice. I glanced at Milgazia.

"Did you just say something?" I asked him, although I half knew the answer.

He shook his head. "No. That was likely the 'voice' of the Claire Bible; I heard nothing at all."

*So the orb can talk.* Yeah, it was a weird day.

If Milgazia hadn't heard anything, then that meant the voice was communicating directly through my head. I took a breath and touched the orb again.

Now *I* didn't hear anything, either. I was starting to get frustrated. Why the heck was the orb clamming up now?!

"Because there is nothing you wish to know," the orb answered calmly.

I jumped. Shaking my head as my heart raced, I decided to try talking to the orb directly.

"You surprised me," I murmured. "And I'm starting to think you, uh . . . Claire Bibles give out their information as answers to asked questions, is that right?"

"Correct," the Bible answered.

Okay—that was easy enough to do. If Milgazia couldn't hear the Claire Bible's voice, a question-and-answer session with the orb would probably look really bizarre to him, but whatever. I'd been psyched out repeatedly since we'd entered that weird place, so trying to avoid looking stupid was already a lost cause.

So that cinched it: I'd ask the questions out loud. Thinking them in my head was probably fine, but it was easier to focus if I said them.

"I have a lot to ask," I began. "But before anything else, can you tell me what Hellmaster Phibrizzo's planning right now?"

"That is not possible," the Bible replied.

*Figures.* And it looked like the Bible was blunt, too.

"It is not possible to convey the thoughts of other beings," the Bible explained. "Only to convey knowledge."

I decided to ask the next question, the most important question, in my head. I braced myself.

*. . . I want to know everything possible about the Lord of Nightmares.*

It was the main reason I'd let Xelloss bring me to the Claire Bible. Coming here had meant Hellmaster could keep his plan, Xelloss could keep me safe from other Mazoku, and I could get the trump card to use when they came after me.

I knew I couldn't beat Xelloss or Hellmaster with the repertoire of spells I had. Milgazia had confirmed that, too, with what he'd said about Xelloss and the dragons. But if I could safely use the spell I'd discovered in Galia years before, drawing on the Demon King among Demon Kings, the Lord of Nightmares . . . then, maybe, *I* could out-power *them*.

Beyond the spell itself, I had no way of learning more specific information about the Lord of Nightmares. Those "Oral Legends of Claire Bible Manuscripts" from Galia had brought me an awful lot of trouble. Even though that trouble had given me two useable, reliable spells and had proved the legends true, I still didn't really know how much trouble I was dealing with.

But now I had the Claire Bible. My information didn't *have* to be scattered anymore.

"That being's so great it's beyond understanding," the Bible answered. "Even what you call 'the Claire Bible' knows only fragments. However, it shall convey the information that it is able to convey."

The Claire Bible started citing a long string of fragmented phrases. "The mother of all darkness, the true lord of all demons, a being with the desire to turn all to the days of yore. An existence darker than darkness and blacker than night; a sea of Chaos, molten gold, complete nothingness . . . that from which all Chaos springs forth. In other words, the Lord of Nightmares."

The voice stopped. I started getting a bad feeling—it felt like something was nagging at me. It was almost like I was misunderstanding something fundamental, maybe.

*One more time, please. I want knowledge on the Lord of Nightmares.*

The Bible recited the same sequence of sentence fragments. I listened more carefully, this time hoping to—

Wait. Wait. Was that it? Maybe . . .

My palms grew sweaty. *One more time,* I requested.

The Bible delivered the same speech. I could feel my heartbeat racing as it reached the end.

". . . In other words, the Lord of Nightmares."

I sucked in a little gasp.

*No,* I thought incredulously. *No, it can't be that.* One by one, I pieced together the fragmented phrases in my head.

*You mean, the Lord of Nightmares is . . .*

"Correct," the Bible replied in response to the murmur of my thoughts.

My knees started to shake. This was insane. Seriously, *seriously*, this was insane.

I'd been casually chanting spells drawing on *that thing's* power?!

I finally understood why Sylphiel had forbidden me from using the magic. Why Xelloss, despite his power, was afraid of me repeating the Lord's name.

It *was* a trump card. But it was a trump card that actually had the potential to—

"Has something happened?" I suddenly heard Milgazia's voice and felt his hand on my shoulder. I gave a start and turned; he was looking down at me in concern.

"What did you hear?" he asked.

I paused a second, then swallowed hard. "Ah," I said with a thin, forced smile. "I, uh . . . hm."

"Are you well? You don't look it."

I gave him a small shrug. "Not really, to be honest. But I'm not quite done." I reached my hand out to the unseen orb again.

Thanks to the Bible's information, now I knew what I *couldn't* use. I still needed something to fight the Mazoku with, though. And then I had all those other things to ask, like how to make Zel human again. I didn't have time to freak out over everything the Bible told me.

*Okay,* I thought. *Next question.*

"Is there some way to exceed the power of demons?" I asked out loud.

The Claire Bible answered with, "To surpass their power, one must possess greater power."

*Huh?* It was a total cop-out answer. I sighed and tried to think of a better way to ask the question.

"Then let me try this," I offered. "How can the one standing before you defeat a demon with immense power?"

"A spell or object drawing on the power of a god or a demon of even greater rank would suffice. But there are limits. And the power of the gods cannot reach this soil, so you cannot use a spell of divine power."

That one threw me a little. "Why not?" I asked.

"When, long ago, a piece of Ruby Eye descended here to destroy the Water Dragon King, his minions—Hellmaster, Deep Sea, Greater Beast, and Dynast—created

SLAYERS: GAAV'S CHALLENGE

a ward to seal divine power at the Desert of Destruction, the Demon Sea, Wolf Pack Island, and the North Pole. The power of the destroyed Water Dragon King, or that of any other Dragon King, cannot reach this place."

Huh. So that's what had happened there.

"Then, um . . . is there any way to defeat a powerful demon with the Sword of Light? Used by a human, I mean."

"'Sword of Light' is the name you use. If you could draw upon the Goln Nova's full power, then—"

The voice suddenly broke off. Without even a word of warning, Milgazia yanked my left hand from behind.

I blurted a sound of protest. But the instant he made my body float back, I realized that something invisible had just moved into where I'd been. A familiar voice came out of nowhere.

"Why do you save her, Gold Dragon elder?" Raltaak asked.

*Dammit!* It was bad news, to say the least. "Raltaak?!" I called as I turned to empty space.

As if responding to my voice, a cloud that vaguely resembled a human shape appeared way to the right of where I'd been looking. "This is quite an odd place,"

Raltaak commented, his form still hazy. "It wasn't easy finding you."

Was that his real form? I also realized that the weirdness of our surroundings was possibly just altering his appearance. Either way, there he was, and that meant I had to deal with him.

He'd known the Claire Bible was our objective. He'd probably come via a different route from a very different place.

"By the way, Gold Dragon elder," Raltaak said with a tone casual enough for a dinner-date. "I'm afraid this girl is being used by Hellmaster, and thus I would like to dispose of her now as a reasonable precaution. You don't object to that, do you?"

Raltaak talking about killing me in the same tone he'd use to order a drink was really starting to piss me off. But I figured I was screwed, since Milgazia probably wouldn't be able to help me.

Believe it or not, Milgazia *did* try to help me. "One thing," he said to Raltaak, "before I reply to your request. If this girl were to choose to oppose Hellmaster and Xelloss, I think it would no longer be necessary to slay her."

"I can't accept that," Raltaak replied. "Without knowing the details of Hellmaster's scheme nor the girl's role in it, there's no telling what sort of damage she may cause. There is even a risk that accepting your proposal may be in accordance with Hellmaster's scheme."

Milgazia deliberated on that one. After a few seconds, he gave a nod.

"I see," he said. "Then I cannot hand her over."

It was the best news I'd heard all day. *Yeah!* I thought triumphantly. *You tell him, you wonderful hunk of mythology!*

"Oh?" Raltaak asked. "And why is that? Surely you're not siding with Hellmaster and Xelloss."

"No. However, Xelloss is at the opening of the path from here to Dragon's Peak. I don't know what he would do were something to happen to the girl; he might well slay my comrades as reparations for my giving you Lina."

"Then give him an excuse," Raltaak answered calmly. "Tell him that I came suddenly and spirited her away."

Milgazia shook his head. "There's another reason why I must refuse."

"And what is that?"

"Your reckless behavior," Milgazia said evenly. "You're willing to slay this girl, ignorant of the circumstances, merely as a precaution."

Raltaak paused. "What if you're mistaken?" he asked.

"I may be, yet I don't care. Your comrade, General Rashatt—he asked if we might battle against the Ruby Eye of Kataart together." Milgazia locked his hard gaze on the hazy priest. "Certainly I believe that if you two, we dragons, elves, and humans banded together, winning may be a possibility. But the incident with this girl has made matters clear to me; you are willing to kill others easily, as a precaution or convenience, and thus wouldn't hesitate to use us as shields for yourself were we to fight against the Demon King of the North.

"In short," he said in closing. "My reasoning behind refusing your request is that I don't care for *your* reasoning."

"Dragon," Raltaak said shortly, "while I would certainly use *humans* as shield, I would not use you."

"It is the same," Milgazia said in a beautiful shoot-down.

Raltaak made a slightly frustrated murmur. "To be blunt, dragon, I do not understand. To battle together is to make use of each others' might; it's inevitable that roles should be assigned according to ability. Humans have numbers but aren't capable of harming demons, and thus are well suited to being shields. In addition, I'm not sure why you care about how we hope to use them."

"The fact that you speak those words so easily is itself the problem. You are hostile toward Ruby Eye at the moment, but you will forever be demons, both with and without a spirit, living to bring destruction. In the end, that is a path we will not walk together.

"There is an even greater reason why you will not slay this girl: she wishes to live. That is the greatest factor."

Raltaak made another murmuring sound. "So be it," he said at last. "Then I have no choice but to eliminate her without your consent."

I was pretty sure that signified the end of their philosophical argument. *Time to start punching,* I thought.

The concept of a fight in that place with those guys was unsettling. Would I even be included? They'd talked about me plenty, but neither of them had looked at me during most of their argument.

But first, believe it or not, the guys started *trash-talking* each other.

"Do you have some means of stopping me?" Raltaak asked, his tone almost as brush-off as always. "Perhaps you intend to sacrifice your own body."

"No," Milgazia replied. "There is always a way, and a hope, no matter how faint they may be."

. . . Okay, so maybe that one was a little too inspirational to be trash-talk.

"Oh ho," Raltaak hummed. "Do show me, then."

"There is not much to see. Only my doing this."

The words had barely come out of his mouth before Milgazia dropped my hand, slapped a palm on my back, and shoved me. I stumbled a few steps in surprise.

"What?" I blurted as I regained my footing and whipped around. I blinked.

The three of them were gone. No Raltaak, no Milgazia, no Claire Bible.

"Um, hello?" I stared into space for a second, really confused. I eventually realized that Milgazia had probably made *me* disappear as opposed to the other way around. It explained why he'd shoved me all of a sudden, at least.

But that left me with a serious problem: now I was alone in the Maze of Crazy, a place where even Mazoku got lost. Maybe that would make it harder for Raltaak to find me, and it would definitely deter the priest from starting a fight with Milgazia alone, but it still left me lost in the *Maze of Crazy.*

*Great,* I thought sarcastically. *Now what do I do?*

I tried to think logically about how to get out of the illogical setting. Milgazia had said he only knew the way in and the way out—that probably meant he didn't know where I was now. And since he was always talking about hope and believing in yourself and stuff, he probably expected me to find my own way out. I definitely *hoped* that wasn't the case; I literally couldn't tell up from down in that place, and I doubted I could wing it like a demon could.

But if demons *could* do it . . . maybe that meant he'd send a demon to find me? Maybe he'd go back to the entrance and send in Xelloss. If that was the plan, I had plenty of time to wander around blindly. Not my favorite pastime, I'll admit.

I hoped Milgazia was fast. Raltaak was probably looking for me, too, and Xelloss being a stronger demon meant nada if Raltaak got a good enough head start. Milgazia had to go back to the entrance for Xelloss, and that might take—

"This way," Xelloss suddenly called out of thin air.

I blinked. I hadn't been standing there and thinking *that* long, had I?

"Huh?" I looked around, but I didn't see him. I even closed my eyes to try that trick—but still, no Xelloss. The only thing I was sure of was what direction his voice had come from.

It all felt too fast. If time was messed up in that place, I *really* hoped I hadn't been lost for days on the outside or anything.

"Xelloss?" I called back.

"This way," he repeated instead of answering me.

I hesitated. That was definitely Xelloss' voice, but demons could easily mimic voices. I was afraid of following "Xelloss" and ending up at Raltaak.

*You can't worry about too many "what-ifs," Lina,* I reminded myself.

*You can when you're nearly killed about a million times a day,* I retorted.

I sighed. *Get off your ass and go.*

With that decided, I followed the direction of the repeating voice. I eventually realized that I was no longer seeing things like the rock walls and stuff that had been around Milgazia—now I was just wandering in pure senselessness. I absently wondered how long I'd been doing that.

Suddenly, someone grabbed my hand. A figure in black appeared in front of me.

"Well done," Xelloss said. He smiled his little smile.

I sighed in relief. "You're pretty fast," I remarked.

"I came as soon as I heard from Mister Milgazia. You seem to be safe." He raised his eyebrows. "And Mister Raltaak . . . ?"

I shook my head. "He may be around here, but I have no idea."

"Ah. Well, then let's get you back to the others for now."

I furrowed my eyebrows. "Then we're done with the Claire Bible?"

Xelloss shrugged cheerfully. "I don't know. But I brought you to it, and I have no further orders, so that part of my job is done."

*Not really into your job, are ya?*

"I dunno," I said. "I had more things to ask the Bible." It had gotten cut off when talking about the Sword of Light, and I hadn't had the chance to even *ask* about Zel.

"Allow me to be blunt," Xelloss said. "If Mister Rashatt and Mister Raltaak both come into this space at the same time, I may not be able to protect you. In normal space, you have means of escaping or fighting, but we could easily be separated here—and one of them may find you before I do."

*Crap.*

As much as I wanted to go back to the Bible, Raltaak was possibly still lurking around it somewhere. And Xelloss was right about me being screwed if I got lost again.

"Fine," I murmured at last. "Let's get back for now."

Xelloss smiled. "Well, then."

I let him lead me by the hand in whatever non-direction we were going. It wasn't long before the current landscape suddenly became more defined and a faint light hit my eyes.

We were back on the rocky mountain path. My party was there, just like I'd left them.

"Hi," I said with a wave.

"Lina!" Gourry cried, running up to meet me. "Are you okay?!"

I smiled. "Xelloss and Mister Milgazia took care of me. I couldn't look into everything I wanted to because that prick Raltaak butted in, but them's the breaks." I crossed my arms confidently. "I'll go back when things calm down a little. It's not like the Claire Bible's going any—"

"Get down!" Gourry suddenly knocked me to the floor.

KA-BOOOM!

An explosion erupted from inside the cliff that acted as the Bible entrance. Giant pieces of rubble were deflected before they could rain down on us; it looked like Xelloss and Milgazia had raised defensive spell barriers immediately.

*What now?!* I thought angrily. *Cut me some slack—I just got here!*

As the roar of the explosion finally trailed off, a lone silhouette walked out of the lingering dust. Three guesses who it was, and here's your hint: HE SUCKS.

Xelloss coughed into a fist. "You're really being very persistent this time, Mister Raltaak."

"Mm . . . it seems that I can dally here no longer." Raltaak looked unusually serious. "I think it's time that we settled this. Wouldn't you agree, Sir Xelloss?"

Xelloss smiled. "I wouldn't mind that at all, Mister Raltaak, Mister Rashatt."

*Rashatt?*

"You seem confident," Rashatt suddenly said from behind us. I whipped my head to him.

I didn't know when he'd gotten there, but there he was. He was wearing his dragon armor and carried his sword in one hand. Since he was behind us and Raltaak was in front, our group was essentially penned in.

"My abilities have fully recovered from your assault," Rashatt announced. "Who knows how the match might proceed?" He glanced at Milgazia. "Gold Dragon elder, surely you won't raise a hand against us?"

Milgazia returned Rashatt's look with a chilling gaze of his own. "That was never my intention from the beginning," he replied promptly. "I simply refuse to participate in a dispute among demons if it results in the one-sided slaughter of the powerless."

Powerless? For a fleeting instant, I realized he was talking about saving me at the Claire Bible—and I bristled a little at the connotation that I'm weak. But, to be fair, I wasn't really on Raltaak's level . . . and compared to dragons and demons, humans can't do much.

*Man,* I thought. *Maybe I should hang out with a less apocalyptic crowd.*

"If possible, I don't wish to raise a hand against you, either," Raltaak said as he looked at us lowly humans. "But if Xelloss loses, I'm afraid you'll be next. You *did* assist Xelloss in interfering with Sir Rashatt and me."

He thrust his right hand out in front of him, the palm facing down. "Since I don't wish to waste effort on you," he continued, "this opponent will take care of you while we settle things with Xelloss."

A black hole suddenly popped open from the rocky ground below his palm. A pair of balls—one pale gray, the other vivid red—slowly floated up to hover unsteadily in front of Raltaak. Each ball was about as big around as the circumference of my arms.

I knew the real form of those things. I narrowed my eyes at Raltaak.

"More Mazoku, huh?"

"That is correct." The balls quivered in front of Raltaak, hovering about as high as his chest. "They may not appear to be much, but they're mightier than your earlier opponents, Gduza and Dugld. They would introduce themselves if they could hear or speak to humans."

"Look at me caring," I snapped. "We're not gonna know them for long, anyway."

"I suppose not. Well, then." At Raltaak's verbal signal, bloodlust blanketed the area.

I clenched my fists. *Bring it on, baby.*

# 4: THE DEMON DRAGON KING REVEALS HIMSELF

General Rashatt was the first to move. It looked like he didn't intend to shift to an Astral Plane battlefield again—he charged straight at Xelloss with his sword in hand, simultaneously releasing a walnut-sized energy ball from his free palm.

Xelloss smiled and swung his arms.

CLANG!

Rashatt's sword met Xelloss' clerical staff. At the same moment, the mantle Xelloss had swung to catch the energy ball flapped back down to his feet, the ball successfully snuffed.

*Whoa.* It was pretty impressive.

Rashatt and Xelloss started going at it after that, sending sparks flying from their collisions and blowing holes in the ground with their missed spells. Despite the chunks of earth and rock they kept sending into the air, their fight was pretty conservative; they were consciously reducing the aftereffects of their powers. If they'd really wanted to let loose, they probably could've leveled the entire area.

It made sense, though. They were avoiding risks and wastes of energy, plus Xelloss didn't want to accidentally vaporize us and Rashatt didn't want to hurt and thus piss off the dragons. The two of them mostly stuck to blocking hits and neutralizing magic.

It also looked like they were using the Astral Side a little. I could only see it in bits and pieces, but . . . for a second, a black haze appeared and then disappeared over Raltaak's head. His sword shook slightly and he let out a groan. I could guess how the fight was going, but I had no idea of the specifics.

*Sure, Lina. Very cool—now could you go fight your own demons, please?!*

The smart part of my brain reminded me that Raltaak's demon balls were coming straight for me. They were slow, and looked pretty silly (especially the cherry tomato one), but I knew better than to underestimate demons. And Raltaak was probably the kind of Mazoku who used power from the Astral Plane left and right.

I glanced over at Amelia and Zelgadiss. They hadn't been with Gourry and me when we'd fought against that sort of thing in Saillune, so they looked pretty freaked.

"Careful!" I called to them. "No matter how stupid those things look, they're probably pretty tough!"

Amelia frowned nervously. "I know, but . . ."

"I already hate them," Zelgadiss said flatly.

The two of them began chanting spells. I started my own chanting as Gourry drew the Sword of Light.

Amelia threw open her palms. "Elmekia Lance!" she cried.

The second Amelia shot off her spell, the gray ball suddenly moved itself in front.

SHWOOP!

The damn thing *absorbed* the lance of light. And the same moment it did that, the red ball shot several of its own lances of light at Zelgadiss.

Zelgadiss was ready. "Astral Vine!" he shouted.

As the spell he'd chanted infused his sword with magic energy, he leapt over a few of the spears and parried the rest with his blade.

*My turn.* "Dark Claw!"

I sent a formless mass of black magic energy—like a swarm of insects—straight for the red ball. The gray one flew at a surprisingly fast speed to get in front.

SHWOOP!

The gray ball sucked up the spell as the red one released a black mist.

*Uh-oh.*

"Duck!" I shouted as I dove behind a rock outcropping. Gourry, Amelia, and Zel landed behind me a second later.

I could hear the sound of liquefying earth as the spell hit the rock. When the four of us poked our heads over to look, I noticed a ton of small, shallow holes scattered across the stone.

My eyes widened. Was that . . . the Dark Claw spell?!

*So that's it!* I thought. The gray ball was taking the hits, and the red ball was amplifying and returning them. Those sneaky little bastards.

"Everybody aim for the red one!" I shouted.

"Got it." Gourry leapt out from behind the outcropping and charged the red ball with his Sword of Light. Before he could get to it, though, the red ball shot arrows of light at him while the gray ball moved in to block.

Gourry easily knocked the arrows away and slid past the gray ball. The red ball flew back in a hurry, getting out of sword range before it slowed to a halt.

Sword range doesn't matter to Gourry. In a very slick move, he shot the blade of the Sword of Light at the red ball.

That was when the red ball faded into a gray color and the gray ball turned red. The balls actually *switched*.

SHWOOP!

The gray-ized ball took the hit as the red-ized one shot multiple light blades. Since the gray ball Gourry had dodged was the one that was now red, that put those shooting blades headed directly for his back.

Gourry whipped around, but it was already too late to dodge.

"Gaav Flare!"

Amelia's hellish flames tore through the air, absorbing the light blades. They always say—a good offence can make the best defense.

Gourry quickly put some distance between himself and the now-red ball. "Thanks, Amelia!" he called.

Meanwhile, I was starting to formulate a hypothesis on the balls. The fact that they could switch colors *and* properties made me wonder if they were two parts of the same demon instead of two separate demons. Their connection seemed a little too deep for different creatures.

*And maybe his real body's on the Astral Plane,* I thought. *He could be materializing offensive-only and defensive-only parts here.*

Unfortunately, the balls didn't want to give me time to think things out. Their next move was ignoring Gourry and coming straight for *me.*

*Which means I'm their real target,* I added to my stockpile of observations.

"I think we have to hit them both at the same time!" Amelia called to me.

Zel moved out from beside Amelia and me and looped around the side. "I'll take the flank," he offered.

That was when the balls, already flying toward me, picked up speed and shot simultaneous lighting bolts.

"H-hey!" Amelia and I barely dodged. The balls didn't pause for a second—they just continued to barrel down on us.

I finished chanting my spell. I quickly glanced at Zel, and he threw me a nod.

*Here goes.*

"Elmekia Lance!" we shouted together.

Our lances of light screamed through the air, each aimed for a different ball. But before they could impale the balls, something invisible deflected them.

I cursed. The balls didn't just reflect attacks— apparently, they could block if they had to.

The two balls picked up speed in their charge, looking ready to run me over. I started chanting my next spell as fast as I could in a desperate attempt to beat them to the finish.

I didn't have to. "Visfrank!" Amelia boomed.

BOOF!

Amelia socked the red ball with her magically reinforced fist. Since it obviously hadn't expected to get *punched*, the ball went careening in another direction.

It was classic Amelia. Of all the people in the world, I was pretty sure she and her father were the only humans capable of laying a physical smack down on a Mazoku. Well . . . them, and one other girl I knew.

*Knock him dead, Amelia!*

Amelia didn't let up; as the red ball was blown back, she chased after it to keep wailing on it. The two balls made a noise that sounded like gold coins jingling.

That cinched it—the demons were a single being. As Amelia pressed in on the red ball, the gray one charged for her back.

SHINK.

A single blow from Zel's magically infused broadsword split the gray ball in two.

That was when the balls exploded.

\*\*\*

"Nngh . . ." I moaned, my eyelids slowly cracking open.

The first thing I noticed was a small rock digging into the back of my head. I grunted and rolled over, trying to remember where I was.

The last things I'd seen had been the two demon balls exploding. My hearing was still a little dulled from the noise, and my body hurt in a few spots, but nothing seemed serious. I was pretty sure I'd only been under momentarily.

*Amelia. Zel.*

My eyes snapped open fully. Unlike me, they'd been at point-blank range during the explosions—which meant they'd taken even harder hits than I had. I jerked my head up in the same instant that I scrambled to my knees.

I could see them. They were at base of a battered wall of rock nearby, sprawled out on the littered ground.

*Dammit!*

"Amelia!" I shouted as I stumbled over. "Zel! Are you guys okay?!"

I saw Zelgadiss slowly move so he could clutch at his temple with a moan. But Amelia, for her part, wasn't even twitching.

*Dammit!* I dropped to my knees the instant I reached her. "Amelia!" I screamed at her as I grabbed her wrist for a pulse.

She was alive. Up close, I could see that she was breathing.

I let out the breath I'd unintentionally been holding. She was alive, which was good, but her injuries looked serious. She needed a Recovery spell.

*But will it work?* I wondered. In exchange for healing injuries, that spell sapped a patient's endurance; it was hard to tell whether or not Amelia's body would give out before she could get better. A Resurrection spell would have been a better idea, since it drew small portions of the vitality of things in the vicinity.

Whatever I did, I had to do it fast—she wouldn't last long the way she was. It was too late for regrets.

I quickly licked my lips and started chanting a spell.

"That will likely be too late."

I stopped and looked up. Milgazia, still in human form, kneeled down next to me.

"Mister Milgazia?" I breathed.

He placed his hands over Amelia's body. An inhuman sound hit the wind, an apparent piece of some spell.

Amelia's wounds literally started closing before my eyes. I had to blink once to make sure I wasn't seeing things.

*Oh, man.* Whatever he was using, it was more powerful than Resurrection.

"Y-you're helping us?" I asked, not really sure what else to say.

Milgazia gazed down at Amelia. She was still pale, but she was definitely better.

"So long as you are not my enemies," Milgazia murmured, "I have no reason to abandon those in need."

I swallowed hard. "Um . . . thanks."

I turned to check on Zel. It looked like the rocky hide he hated so much had, once again, saved his hide. His injuries hadn't been that serious, and he'd apparently already used Recovery on himself.

Noticing my glance, he sent me a small nod. It was Zelgadiss code for *I'll be fine.*

Gourry—who hadn't been hit by the explosion, by the way—ran up at that point, panting. "Are you guys okay?" he asked quickly. "You got hit pretty bad. How's Amelia?"

I gestured to her and the dragon. "Mister Milgazia's taking care of her."

Gourry sighed in relief. "That's good," he said, looking over Amelia's prone form.

Most of my dizziness from being thrown had subsided, so I started to mentally work through our situation. Up until then, no Mazoku we'd ever fought had exploded at time of death. That was probably a Raltaak feature, considering how much the guy got off on contingency plans.

Raltaak had miscalculated—the explosion hadn't been powerful enough to do us in. Of course, that didn't make me feel much better about Amelia and Zel taking the hit for me.

Raltaak was gonna pay for *that* one.

"Gourry," I said as I stood. "Lend me the Sword of Light."

"Right." He tossed the Sword of Light to me with the blade extinguished. I caught it, poised it with my right hand, and shifted my eyes to Xelloss and Raltaak's ongoing battle.

That bastard was mine. Yeah, I was a little mad that I was neatly falling into Xelloss' plan, but I was willing to do that to take down that old son of a bitch.

It was time for the Dragon Slave Blade.

*"Thou who art darker than night,*

*Thou who art redder than the flowing blood,*

*Thou through whom time flows, I call upon thy exalted name . . ."*

Halfway through chanting my spell, I saw that Raltaak, on Xelloss' right side, had noticed what I was doing.

The Dragon Slave. Invoked by a human, it was an offensive spell that called upon the power of the Demon King Ruby Eye Shabranigudu. It was possibly capable of affecting a demon of Raltaak's rank, but it definitely wouldn't be enough.

That was where the Sword of Light came in. I'd only done it once before, but casting Dragon Slave on the sword made a blade of crimson light that was *very* destructive. That was what I wanted to sink into Raltaak.

He probably hadn't guessed my intentions that far, but he still tossed a small ball of magic energy in my direction . . . as a *precaution*, knowing him.

*Dammit!*

I knew I could probably strike it down, but at the same time I had no idea how powerful it was—for all I knew, hitting the stone-sized object could trigger another explosion. But at the same time, if I dodged, the ball would shoot past me and put everyone behind me in danger again.

I decided on Option A. Before I could go through with it, though, the energy ball vanished into thin air.

Xelloss again, probably. Raltaak looked miffed.

I completed my spell. "Dragon Slave!" I cried.

Reacting to the Power Words, a blade of scarlet light sprung from the Sword of Light. I gripped it tightly in my right hand and charged Raltaak at full speed.

Raltaak, still looking pissed, suddenly expanded his will. The gust of intense power made me screech to a stop.

His will took on a tangible energy, like miasma. Although it wasn't so intense that I couldn't grit my teeth and push through, his constantly pouring it out could make me collapse in exhaustion before I got to him.

I wielded the sword in both hands, straight against the pressure. "Go!" I shouted.

The crimson blade obeyed my voice and mind and shot out toward Raltaak.

*Get him!* my brain screamed.

Raltaak cursed. He was just about to dodge when something huge and black impaled his stomach.

A dark corkscrew.

"GAAAAAAH!" Raltaak screeched, no longer moving out of the way.

In a ray of burning red light, my blade slammed into his chest. As Raltaak reeled, gurgling, another corkscrew suddenly appeared and smashed his head into little bits.

That, obviously, was the last of Priest Raltaak.

Raltaak's form scattered in all directions, sounding like an apple being crushed by a hammer. All that remained where he'd been standing was a puddle of blackish-blue liquid that was quickly absorbed by the earth and dissolved by the wind.

I swallowed. Xelloss, his unchanging smile on his face, and a stunned General Rashatt were the only ones left standing on the battlefield.

"S-sir Raltaak!" Rashatt gasped. He slowly turned his wide eyes to Xelloss.

Xelloss tapped the bottom of his staff on the ground. "Now, then," he said cheerfully.

That was as far as he got. Rashatt vanished that instant, leaving only his pathetic scream behind.

I lowered my arms and sighed. Xelloss, scratching his nose, stood there in silence a second.

"He got away pretty easily," he finally commented absentmindedly.

I snorted. "Well, duh!" I snapped across the field. "And good job trying to stop him there, genius!"

Xelloss brushed a strand of hair behind his ear. "Er . . . at any rate, things seem to be in order. Thank you very much for your assistance, Miss Lina." He glanced at me. "Your distracting of Mister Raltaak was particularly helpful. It was getting dangerous there, I must admit.

"So . . ." He raised his eyebrows. "Is everyone all right?"

That snapped me back to reality. Why was I arguing with Xelloss when I had party members recovering?! I spun around and ran back to the others.

Gourry was crouched next to Zelgadiss. I quickly gave Gourry back his sword and looked down at Zel.

"You okay?" I asked him. "By the way—thanks, Gourry."

Zelgadiss shook his head. "It's not serious," he murmured, his voice tired but regaining its usual edge. "For me, anyway. How's Amelia?"

I deflected the question to Milgazia. The Gold Dragon elder nodded.

"The healing is complete," he said calmly. "She should be fine now."

Sure enough, when I checked on Amelia I could see her breathing normally. She was still unconscious, but her wounds were completely closed.

Relief flooded through me. *That's one cool spell*, I thought. I nodded at Milgazia in appreciation.

"Thanks a lot, Mister Milgazia."

He abruptly averted his eyes. "There's no need to thank me," he declared curtly.

I stopped for a second. If I didn't know better, I could've sworn the guy was embarrassed.

"By the way," he muttered, cutting off my thoughts. "It seems the door has vanished."

"Door?" I followed his eyes. To the right of the rocky, imposing path that led up to the peak, a large portion of the cliff had been gouged out of the mountain.

*Crap!*

"Not the door to the Claire Bible?!" I exclaimed, hoping beyond hope that I was wrong.

"Precisely."

"You're kidding me!" I ran up and tried putting my hand through the gouged-out cliff where the Bible door would have been. My body had gone straight through before, but this time I just skinned my knuckles and looked like a moron.

It was one of the worst disappointments *ever*.

It had probably happened because Raltaak had caused an explosion inside that space. Stupid, stupid Raltaak!

I whimpered. "Does this mean . . . the Claire Bible's gone, too?"

"This door was not the only one leading to the distortion at the center," Milgazia said in reply. "Surely that energy was insufficient to cause the distortion that is the Claire Bible to vanish. However, not even I know if the vanishing of the door might have some effect upon the Bible."

I dropped my hand and sighed. So much for asking about the Sword of Light or Zel's chimera problem. I could go searching for another door, maybe, but I had no idea where to even start.

But that did make me think of something. If Xelloss knew that there were other doors to the Claire Bible, maybe he knew where to find another one.

I turned to him. "Xelloss?" I asked. "Do you know any other places to get to the Bible?"

He made a face. "Er . . . I know of a few, I suppose, but they're in difficult places and, um, I can't tell you where they are."

*Jerk.*

"Why not?!" I asked angrily. I could guess the reason, but I still figured I'd ask.

"Why . . . ?" Xelloss raised his eyebrows again. "My duty was to bring you to this Claire Bible, after all. And now that this door is gone, others will be upset with me if I just bring you along to another one."

I scoffed. "You just don't like having to use your delicate hands for real work."

"I'm following orders, which I'm sure I've mentioned. We demons have absolute obedience to those above us; in this case, Mister Raltaak and Mister Rashatt became our enemies because Chaos Dragon Gaav ordered them to act as such."

I thought on that one for a minute.

SLAYERS: GAAV'S CHALLENGE

"But if demons have absolute obedience to their superiors," I asked, "why did Gaav turn against Ruby Eye? Ruby Eye created him."

Xelloss started walking down the slope at a casual pace. "Ah," he replied. "There are some special circumstances with that one. First of all, the Demon War of over a millennium ago was the cause of many unusual events. At the time, both Ruby Eye and Chaos Dragon confronted the Water Dragon King—but when the Water Dragon King was destroyed, Chaos Dragon was felled, seemingly by a mutual strike.

"Well," Xelloss added to clarify, "by *felled* I don't mean *destroyed*. His power was temporarily sealed along with any and all means by which he could interact with the world. Normally, left to his own devices, he would have revived on his own."

*Wow.* "Your kind revives like that?" I asked.

"It depends on the individual's power and the circumstances of defeat. The term *destroyed* means that all abilities, willpower, memories, and soul have been torn into small pieces so that even if the power *were* to shift elsewhere—and there may indeed be cases like that—the being will nonetheless never regain original form.

"Normally, being *defeated* means being unable to materialize power in this world. But, either through the passage of time or the recovery of one's power through some means, the being will once again be able to materialize in the world at some point."

Zelgadiss was finally on his feet by the time Xelloss arrived. Xelloss stopped in the area next to Zel before continuing with his piece.

"For some reason," Xelloss went on, "there seem to be many instances of low-ranking demons, like lesser demons and brass demons, reviving in some incomplete form that cannot be called demonic. But power such as that possessed by Chaos Dragon should eventually revive in full.

"So. Where was I?" Xelloss cleared his throat. "The Water Dragon King placed an unusual seal on Chaos Dragon. Just before being destroyed, he used a fragment of his own mind as a key and reincarnated Chaos Dragon within a human body; it was a sort of spell that worked on other dragons, most likely.

"However, the spell was apparently not complete. As his spirit was reincarnated again and again, Chaos Dragon regained his memory and abilities. It would have been fine if it had ended there, but . . ."

Fine? *By whose standards?* I wanted to ask. From the standpoint of a human being, that situation was definitely *not* fine.

"While reincarnating many times over—possibly with the Water Dragon King's mind fragment as a catalyst—part of the revived Chaos Dragon's soul became humanized. Although a Mazoku's characteristics are fundamentally stronger, because of the human sensibilities mixed in, he quickly rebelled from Lord Ruby Eye. He even took the subordinates he created long ago and began to take an antagonistic posture."

Xelloss sighed. "I must say," he said sadly. "The youths of today can be such a hassle."

"Um . . ." I made a face. "Chaos Dragon is *young?*"

Xelloss waved a hand dismissively and smiled. "I meant it as a figure of speech. In any case, in order to survive in spite of his betrayal, he's rallied part of the demon population to his side against Lord Ruby Eye—as futile a cause as that may seem.

"The Demon Lord of North Kataart is the only piece of Lord Ruby Eye that has currently materialized in this world. If something were to happen to him, the demons would lose their focal point and could do as they pleased. That, you see, would improve Chaos Dragon's chance at survival."

Xelloss tapped a lip with his finger. "It seems that he intended to gather dragons and elves, invade the Kataart Mountains, and, in the midst of the chaos, defeat Lord Ruby Eye. Lord Ruby Eye is still partially sealed by the Water Dragon King and is unable to wield his full power."

"A plan you easily foiled," commented a voice from behind me.

I spun around. Rashatt, wielding his drawn sword, glared at Xelloss and me.

I carefully spread my feet. *Look who came crawling back.*

"Mister Rashatt!" Xelloss called in a conversational tone. "I see you've come back to join us."

Rashatt set his jaw. "Now that Sir Raltaak has been defeated," he murmured, "I cannot win against you alone. But I can dispose of the girl, at the very least."

*Easier said that done, pal!*

Xelloss shrugged. "I understand how you feel, of course, but I'm afraid—"

His words were suddenly interrupted by Gourry shouting his name.

Some kind of presence flooded in. Xelloss, his eyelids flying up in uncharacteristic shock, spun around on his heel.

A red flash originated out of thin air and split the sky. Almost as if the world had been set to slow motion, I watched as that flash sliced off Xelloss' right arm at the shoulder.

I froze. Before I could even register the insanity I'd just witnessed, a second, horizontal strike split open Xelloss' belly. The lopped-off arm turned into black mist and vanished before it could hit the ground.

*What the HELL?!*

Xelloss choked back a noise and made a long backward leap. The wounds didn't seem to be fatal, but his knees still buckled the moment he landed.

"Xelloss!" I screamed. I ran over to him before I realized what I was doing.

*That attack,* I thought in a daze. *It came out of nowhere, like Xelloss' corkscrews!*

"I thought attacks from the Astral Plane were *your* specialty, Priest of the Beast God."

The voice was deep and male. I turned my head to see a man in the direction opposite to Rashatt, seemingly blocking the path that continued up to the peak.

The guy didn't look older than twenty. He had a solid build, long red hair blown back by the wind, and an ivory white coat wrapped around his big frame. He tapped his own shoulder with the flat of a crimson-bladed long sword he gripped with his right hand.

He was handsome, in a rugged way, but the broad smile on his face was wicked.

"It's . . . been some time," Xelloss gasped from his crouched position on the ground. "We meet again, Chaos Dragon Gaav."

Chaos Dragon.

*Chaos Dragon.*

I stared in morbid fascination. No wonder Rashatt had come back—the big baby had brought his boss with him.

"It has," Gaav agreed casually. "Since before the Demon War, was it?" He passed Gourry, who was in a fighting stance, and me, before stopping in front of Xelloss.

Since Xelloss was a demon, he wasn't losing blood or anything—there was just a smooth, white surface where his arm used to be attached his shoulder. But blood or no, he'd taken some serious damage.

"You've certainly changed in the millennium since I last saw you, Demon Dragon King."

Gaav raised an eyebrow. "Really." he said. "Was I more polite in the old days?"

"The opposite, actually. Your temper was a little shorter."

Gaav smiled at that. "You're still alive after taking two hits from me. You live up to my expectations, Priest Xelloss. To be blunt, the same attack would have destroyed Rashatt or Raltaak."

Rashatt, obviously, didn't look happy to hear that. But I guess he knew well enough to keep his mouth shut.

"You won't get over those wounds for a while," Gaav went on. "You'll recover your strength given time, though."

"Mm," Xelloss agreed. "And I've lost so much strength that even Mister Rashatt may be able to defeat me in a fight."

"I resent that!" Rashatt retorted from the back. Nobody seemed to care.

"It's been busy around here." Gaav tapped his shoulder with his sword again. "On top of your ridiculous scheme, you defeated Raltaak—and after we went through all the trouble to stay secret and not harm humans. Losing out on the power of Galia does hurt, I must admit."

I couldn't keep quiet anymore. That arrogant prick was one arrogant prick too many.

"What the *hell* are you talking about?!" I shouted. I got to my feet and pointed at Rashatt. "He's the one who burned the place to the ground while trying to get rid of me!"

The Demon Dragon King raised an eyebrow and slowly turned to me. "What are you talking about?" he asked.

Rashatt scowled. "I see you haven't realized," he told me flatly. "The one who burned Galia was none other than Xelloss."

*Huh?*

All the thoughts went flying out of my head. I looked dumbly down at Xelloss, but he just smiled his usual, cryptic smile.

I tried to find something to say. "But . . ." was all I managed.

"I'll explain it to you, young lady." Rashatt kept his eyes locked on me. "My duty was to gain the assistance of elves and dragons for Dilse. Eliminating you was the duty of Sir Raltaak. When I learned that you had come to the city, at the risk of sounding rude, I intended to seize the opportunity to try and kill you.

"But it wasn't *immediate,* this plan. As I told you at the palace, I wanted you to teach the soldiers how to use spells against low-ranking demons. I didn't intend to dispose of you until *after* you'd finished your work."

*What a sweetheart! He didn't want to kill me until* after *wringing out a few weeks of free labor.*

I was really, *really* getting sick of those Mazoku.

"But before that could happen, Xelloss altered his form and voice and pretended to target your life. He destroyed the palace and the city in his pursuit of you. What motive would I have to do that, I ask? We wanted to destroy you, but not at the cost of our bigger plan; as we've mentioned, knowing you're a part of Hellmaster's scheme means we want to kill you as a *precaution,* not as a priority."

As much as I hated to admit it, he had a point. I stared at Xelloss and swallowed hard.

"Xelloss?" I asked, my voice breaking a little.

He stayed completely silent. That was all the proof I needed.

I couldn't believe it. *Everything* had been a part of his plan—he'd manipulated me into destroying Chaos Dragon's military resources and then had gotten me to hate Rashatt and Raltaak for it. I'd meant to dance along to his little tune for a while, but he'd had me flailing stupidly on puppet strings.

"And there you have it," Xelloss said calmly.

ARGH! And the guy didn't even have the decency to have a tone other than *tranquil!*

Xelloss slowly pushed himself to his feet. "I take back . . . what I said," he told Gaav. "Your short temper hasn't changed at all."

Gaav smiled evilly. "Really."

Without batting an eye, Gaav shoved the tip of his sword into Xelloss' abdomen.

"It's time to confess," he drawled. "What scheme is that bastard Hellmaster up to?"

Xelloss didn't change his story. "Regrettably . . . Lord Hellmaster didn't tell me . . . the objective of his plan."

"Then I'll rephrase the question." Gaav tried. "Did you hear the details of the plan from *someone other than Hellmaster?* For example, Greater Beast?"

I croaked out my surprise in a weird gurgle. No way. *NO WAY.*

Xelloss had never actually said "I don't know."

Xelloss gave Gaav a pained smile. "You get to . . . the point," he huffed around the sword digging into his body. "As you surmised, yes . . . Lord Greater Beast, Zelas Metallium, did tell me the fine details of this plan. And the plan's objective is . . ."

Gaav leaned in. "Is?" he pushed.

Xelloss smiled and touched his lip. ". . . is . . . a . . . secret."

The instant he said the words, Xelloss vanished without a trace.

Rashatt growled from behind me. "Is he trying to run?"

"After him, Rashatt." Gaav didn't seem bothered. "I'll go later. And I'm sure you can defeat him, considering his condition."

"Yes, sir!" Rashatt vanished in an instant.

Gaav slowly turned in our direction. "Now," he muttered. "As for you, young lady."

I gritted my teeth. He didn't have to say it—I knew he wanted to kill me.

"I still don't know Hellmaster's plan," he admitted, "but I'm killing you anyway. I still want to ruin what Hellmaster's planning *and* pay you back for the trouble you've caused."

"Over my dead body."

I froze. Gourry, the Sword of Light in his hand, slowly walked to stand between Gaav and me.

*Gourry?*

Gaav eyed the sword. "The Goln Nova," he said with interest. "That's quite the toy you have there."

I couldn't believe anyone could call the Sword of Light a *toy*. But that name he'd used, *Goln Nova* . . . those were the same words the Claire Bible had recited.

Gaav shrugged. "No matter how much you wave that, no human can use it to defeat me. Do you honestly want to bet your life on a battle you can't win?"

Gourry smiled. "I'm her guardian," he answered. After a second, he added, "Self-appointed, I guess, but a guardian's still a guardian. I can't let you kill her."

"The same goes for me." Zelgadiss stood painfully on unsteady legs, but he still managed to give Gaav a dark, intense smile.

"I'm not her guardian," he murmured, "but I'm still her companion. I won't watch you kill her, even if I can only manage a few attack spells."

"That's right!" That was *Amelia*, shockingly energetic and opposite Zel. "Where's there's a will, there's a way. And we have the will!"

"Amelia!" I shouted. She was already up and making speeches?!

She seemed completely fine, her chest puffed up and her finger pointed accusingly at Gaav. It was a real sight for sore eyes, let me tell you.

"I don't know how strong you are," she announced, "but if we fight you with everything we have, Justice *will* prevail!"

"Amelia!" I called. "When did you wake up?! Are you okay?"

Amelia scoffed. "Hmph! A blast like that is *nothing* to a heart fueled by *Justice!*"

Maybe she'd forgotten that whole "almost dying" part.

"But more importantly, Lina!" Amelia pointed again at Gaav. "Who is that guy?!"

If people could spontaneously explode, all of us would have right then.

I slapped a hand to my forehead. "Amelia!" I growled. "This isn't the time to pull a Gourry. What part did you wake up at?"

"Um . . . something about not knowing Hellmaster's scheme, but killing you anyway. I figured he was bad, so my Righteous Anger raged!"

I forced myself to swallow all the insults that bubbled up in me; it just wasn't the time. "He's Chaos Dragon!" I exclaimed. "Gaav! Okay? He knocked around Xelloss until Xelloss ran off!"

"Chaos Dragon?" Amelia repeated, her eyebrows raising. "Hm . . . I guess I always thought he'd look scarier than that."

"I hate bluffing," Gaav said dryly. "I could change into a monster, but that wouldn't make me stronger or more frightening. I prefer this form."

Amelia pressed her lips into a tight line. "Regardless! You're the one who plunged the royals of Saillune and Dilse into chaos and is trying to kill Lina! You're a villain, through and through!"

Gaav laughed without humor. "Please," he mocked. "This isn't about good and evil. I'm simply doing what I need to do in order to survive."

"If selfishly dragging everyone into your problems and spreading chaos isn't evil, then what is? HM?!"

Gaav sneered. "All right, then listen. Hellmaster's plan is probably the source of this chaos. If Lina's willing to play along, and you're supporting her, doesn't that make *you* villains?"

Amelia, in a very, *very* rare moment, was struck absolutely speechless.

"What's evil about fighting for survival?" Gaav asked. "Or is it better to be like the demons in Kataart and live solely to destroy everything and everyone?"

Amelia's eyebrows furrowed. "Everything and everyone?" she repeated.

"You heard me. They want to destroy the world, and themselves, and return everything to Chaos. That's what demons want—it's why they were created."

I clenched my hands into fists. *So it's true,* I thought. A demon himself was saying it.

Gaav looked away irritably. "Until a millennium ago," he muttered, "I took that for granted, as well. But while dying and being reborn inside of humans, I've since changed my opinion. I won't go along with the demons of Kataart. And I'd be fine with running if I didn't worry about another fragment of Ruby Eye getting resurrected and bringing about the destruction of the world.

"There's only one way to avoid that: find the fragments of Ruby Eye and destroy them one by one. I intend to start with the Demon King of the North at Kataart."

Gaav turned to me again. "To live," he said lowly, "I'll destroy Ruby Eye. I'll smash the plans of that bastard Hellmaster. And I'll kill you, Lina Inverse."

So that was it. All of it—or most of it, at least—and straight from the dragon's mouth. My head was spinning with all the information that had been thrown at me that day.

"I know you're fighting to stay alive," Gaav added. "You and I are alike in that way. I don't expect you or ask you to roll over and die. Fight me and we'll settle this." He gestured to the others. "And bring your friends, while you're at it."

That said, he hefted his sword in one hand and pointed it at me.

"Then let's do this!" Amelia shouted before immediately chanting a spell.

I could hear it. She was going to cast Ra Tilt, the strongest of the Shamanic Magic spells. It could annihilate a typical demon, but what would it do to Chaos Dragon Gaav?

*I guess we're about to find out,* I thought.

But as Amelia finished chanting, Gaav voiced a sound that was a lot like a whistle.

"Ra Tilt!" Amelia cried.

Amelia released her spell. A pillar of blue flames enveloped Gaav's body, burning until . . .

With a sharp, metallic sound, the pillar of flames broke apart.

Amelia's jaw dropped. "What?!"

I wished I could've said I was surprised. But there's no fun in "I told you so" when you being right means you're also dead meat.

"Taking that squarely would do no more than scratch me," Gaav said flatly. "But since I don't like little pains, I decided to block it."

Amelia could only stare at him dumbly, her mouth hanging open.

Gaav snorted. "In human hands, even Goln Nova would do little to hurt me. If you wanted to defeat me with human bodies, you should've brought along some of those famous Ceipheed Knights."

I made a face at that. *Oh, yeah?*

"The Ceipheed Knights are probably working as part-time waitresses right now," I said dryly.

Gaav ignored me. Probably thought I was crazy.

*Back to business.*

"Gourry!" I yelled. "Let's go!"

"Right!" Gourry caught on, so he readied his sword. I began to chant my spell.

Gaav commented, raising his eyebrows a little. "You should know that won't work."

Of course it wouldn't—not if I launched it at him directly.

He made another whistling sound. Was that how he did defensive spells?

I was done. "Dragon Slave!" I cried as I released.

As my spell activated, Gourry's blade shone crimson. Gaav murmured mild surprise and entered a fighting stance for the first time that day.

It looked like Rashatt hadn't gone into detail about Raltaak's death. That was good news for us.

"So that's your plan," Gaav said. "Interesting . . . I was planning on killing you quickly from the Astral Plane, but drawing this out might be fun."

Gaav faced Gourry, a wicked smile pulling his lips tight. "Let's go!" Gaav called before racing across the ground.

He was *ridiculously* fast. Gourry managed to parry Gaav's sharp, twisting thrust and still stay on his feet. Gaav pushed in and didn't give Gourry any leeway.

CLANG CLANG CLANG!

Shockwaves and red plasma gushed out of the Sword of Light every time it blocked a hit from Gaav's own scarlet sword. It looked like the Sword of Light was losing the most power with every blow; nothing was spilling out of the Chaos Dragon's blade. The fact that Gourry was about equal in sword skill wouldn't mean much if he lost the magic weapon.

I had to work fast. While Gaav was distracted with Gourry, I had time to use a spell . . . but I could only think of one that would do real damage. I didn't want to use it, considering its true nature. I really, *really* didn't. But then who would save Gourry? Or all of us, for that matter?

Then I had an idea. I had that other spell, the one that had less of a chance of running amok. I could use that.

*Do it, Lina!*

I put my hands in front of my chest, my palms slightly apart, like I would to cast a fireball. First, I had to chant the amplification spell. In answer to those Chaos Words, the four Demon Blood Talismans on my two wrists, my belt, and my necklace released pale light in four colors.

I began chanting the main spell, raising my right hand to the sky.

"Fragment of the Lord of Nightmares,

Release thy heavenly retribution

Blade of cold, black nothingness

Become my power, become my body

Together, let us walk the path of destruction

And smash even the souls of the Gods—"

Chaos Dragon stopped in shock. "What?!" he choked out.

Gourry took advantage of the situation and sliced, but he only managed a shallow wound on the retreating Demon Dragon King's chest.

The spell was a version I'd modified using knowledge from the Claire Bible and my own guesswork. It was probably in its complete form.

"Ragna Blade!" I shouted.

VOOOOOO!

The very fabric of space shook as a blade of nihility appeared in my right hand. But something was different this time around—the power wasn't the same as before. It was stronger.

"Huh?!"

I could barely do it. Controlling the blade alone was draining both my physical and mental strength. I wouldn't last long—so I had to make this count.

With a cry, I rushed to the still-trembling Gaav and sliced at him with all I had. He raised his blade to parry, and my eyes went blurry.

It was too exhausting; I could feel all my strength being sucked out of me.

But the second I thought that, the space between the two blades went nuts.

The black sword came down just as it lost its power.

There was no resistance.

Without so much as a sound, the seemingly powerless black blade sliced through Chaos Dragon Gaav's sword and *arm.*

"AAAAAH!"

I barely saw Gaav retreat from me in agony. I'd hit my threshold. The black sword returned to the void once more as my knees buckled beneath me.

My palms slapped against the rocky ground. Panting, drenched in sweat, I fought to stay conscious.

"G-Gourry!" I gasped.

I heard him shout an affirmative. He charged Gaav with his sword.

Gaav roared. His will surged outward, turning into a shockwave that blew Gourry and I back.

I cried out as I rolled over and over before sliding to a halt. I tried to struggle to my feet, but my body had no strength left. I collapsed weakly.

I looked up through blurred eyes. I saw the outline of Gaav slowly walking in my direction. A black *something* was devouring him where his right arm had been cut off.

"I'll kill you!" he shrieked as his red hair fanned out.

The scream of Chaos Dragon Gaav resounded across Dragon's Peak.

**To be continued . . .**

# AFTERWORD

Hajime Kanzaka + "L"

**Author:** Ugh! It's finally out! Slayers novel volume seven, "Gaav's Challenge"!

**L:** Jeez, it sure took you long enough.

**Author:** It did. All that revising took a while.

**L:** Yeah, it took you about five thousand years to get this Slayers novel out.

**Author:** Well . . . that's, er, overstating it a little . . .

**L:** What? It's been about five thousand years since the universe was born, right? Something like that.

**Author:** Like hell it has! Jeez.

**L:** So, it's question time! What was the reason for late publication?

1) Natural disaster

2) Spiritual development

3) Historical inevitability

4) Something in this world that science cannot explain

5) Author incompetence

**Author:** Er . . . um . . .

**L:** You can't wriggle your way out of this one.

**Author:** Well, it's a turning point in the story, you see. I was under a lot of pressure. Back when I was writing volume three, I was still expecting the series to end with the next volume, you see.

**L:** So it's over?

**Author:** Er, well, there was more that I wanted to write, so I decided to keep going.

**L:** You mean you want the story to go on forever, like that Dragon-something-or-other?

**Author:** I don't think you should be talking like that. But anyway, the next story will definitely be a climax. I'll be able to genuinely say, "Part One, Complete" after that.

**L:** Part Two's never gonna start at this rate.

**Author:** Hey! I said don't say stuff like that!

**L:** Well, whether or not Part Two ever comes out, you'd better get the next volume out at least.

**Author:** (Gulp?!)

**L:** Up until now, even the most twisted tale got wrapped up by the end of the book. But this time, you dropped a big, fat "to be continued" on everyone.

**Author:** A-anyway, to make an announcement . . .

**L:** Changing the subject, huh?

**Author:** I still don't have final results ready for the reader popularity contest I wrote about in "Vezendi's Shadow."

**L:** Meaning, the results will be out next time. Probably not in this series, but in Slayers Special instead.

**Author:** A-anyway, um, I'm very grateful for the people at the publisher's who put up with my unilaterally declared popularity contest. But I think there are a fair bunch of entries that never made it to the author here . . .

**L:** I see. So based on the date and what you said . . . You mean by New Year's, right?

**Author:** That's right! I'm really happy to get fan letters like this. The time I spend reading them makes me think, "Yeah! I'm so glad I became an author! I'm a true Tokyoite now, dammit!" and stuff.

**L:** You're a true Tokyoite . . . ?

**Author:** Well, no . . . born in Hyougo, raised in Osaka.

Anyway, I'll count every letter I can get my hands on before New Year's, but it's possible that some letters that don't arrive in time won't get counted. If, by chance, that's the case . . .

**L:** The readers will hate you.

**Author:** Now, now.

**L:** But, there's no way to deal with that now except for saying you're sorry.

**Author:** Well, that's true, so—everyone whose letters didn't arrive by New Year's, sorry. He he he.

**L:** Quit with the heart marks; they're dishonest . . . Oh yeah, by the way, no event this time.

**Author:** Okay!

**L:** You might be tired of these by now.

**Author:** But anyway, see you all here next time!

**L:** Better live up to that . . .

**Author:** Later everyone! Sayonara!

**L:** Don't end it.

**Author:** Come on, let me end it . . .

**L:** (sigh) I guess I gotta. Anyway, that's how it is.

**Author:** So, see you later! As soon as possible!

# Check out the following series also available from TOKYOPOP Fiction:

www.tokyopop.com/popfiction

POP
FICTION